Discovering
Your Soul's Purpose

Discovering Your Soul's

Purpose

Finding Your Path in Life,
Work, and Personal Mission
the Edgar Cayce Way

2nd Edition

Mark Thurston, Ph.D.

A TARCHERPERIGEE BOOK

tarcherperigee

An imprint of Penguin Random House LLC
375 Hudson Street
New York, New York 10014

Printed by arrangement with A.R.E. Press

Tarcher and Perigee are registered trademarks, and the colophon
is a trademark of Penguin Random House LLC.

Most TarcherPerigee books are available at special quantity discounts
for bulk purchase for sales promotions, premiums, fund-raising, and
educational needs. Special books or book excerpts also can be created to fit
specific needs. For details, write:
SpecialMarkets@penguinrandomhouse.com.

ISBN 9780143130857

Printed in the United States of America
1   3   5   7   9   10   8   6   4   2

Contents

Preface to the 2nd Edition

THE PUBLICATION OF this second edition of my 1984 book, *Discovering Your Soul's Purpose*, gives me pause to think about my own engagement with these ideas and principles. I discovered the work and spiritual philosophy of Edgar Cayce when I was a senior in high school—just seventeen and full of wonderings and uncertainties about my own calling and mission in life. Studying and applying these ideas, especially during my college years as I swerved from one academic major to another, profoundly helped me find a direction—a professional focus in psychology, but more important was a direction for the kind of person I aspired to be. Even in this period of my emerging adulthood forty-five years ago, I had already started to appreciate that "discovering your soul's purpose" is more about *being* than *doing*. The doing-ness of a well-chosen occupation was going to be fine, but more critical was finding an optimal way to *be* in life.

The journey to fulfill my own mission took me to Virginia Beach, Virginia. I was given extraordinary opportunities for learning and service as I worked for more than three decades at the very organization that Edgar Cayce had founded in 1931. One tremendous professional gift was the opportunity as a writer and teacher to pick topics from the Cayce material and develop systematic ways that those topics can be studied and applied: dream interpretation, meditation, and the intuitive mind, just to name a few. But for some reason—and maybe it was because of how influential the material had been in my own decision making about my career—I latched on to the Cayce principle that simply states, "For, each soul enters with a mission . . . We all have a mission to perform" (3003-1).* I decided that I wanted to make a truly in-depth study of how Cayce had served as a spiritual director to hundreds of people, helping them to see and claim their own spiritual calling, their personal mission.

As an educator and writer for the Association for Research and Enlightenment (A.R.E.) I had many opportunities to share what I was able to mine from the extensive archival records of Cayce's work as an unconventional, gifted "spiritual psychologist." With my own freshly minted Ph.D. in psychology, I was no doubt overly confident that together

---

* Each of the Edgar Cayce readings has been assigned a two-part number to provide easy reference. Every person who received a reading was anonymously assigned a case number, and this constitutes the first portion of the two-part reading number. The excerpt quoted here was from a reading given for a sixty-one-year-old woman who received the case number 3003. Since many individuals obtained a series of readings over the months or years, the second portion of the reading number indicates what reading it is within the series. Therefore, the notation "-1" denotes here that this was the first reading Cayce gave for this woman.

Edgar Cayce and I could come up with a foolproof system of self-study that would yield a revelation of soul purpose for anyone committed enough to give it a try. I was especially proud of a one-day workshop course that I created, with the same title as this book. This workshop was a full day of experiential learning about oneself, culminating in a guided process to craft the first draft of one's mission statement. A.R.E. conferences sent me to at least forty different cities in the late 1970s and early 1980s to offer the workshop, which probably averaged one hundred people per event. Eventually I presented the program in six other countries. The feedback that I received from many of these thousands of course participants allowed me to refine the presentation and the exercises, and by 1984 the timing seemed right to put these ideas into the original edition of *Discovering Your Soul's Purpose*.

So, why a new edition of this book more than thirty years later? One reason is that there is a growing interest in this theme. Eighty years ago Cayce was one of the few who spoke so specifically and eloquently about each person having a particular soul purpose. Admittedly, there had long been a tradition, especially within Protestant Christianity—which was Cayce's own roots—that everyone could find in his or her occupational work a means to glorify God. In other words, a "calling" was not reserved for those whose vocation was in the church or a religious order. You could be a farmer or a teacher or a business owner and fulfill your calling, *if* you pursued that career with the intention to serve the greater good and glorify the Creator. However, Cayce's spiritual advice to seekers in the 1930s and 1940s helped to pioneer a broader understanding of soul purpose, and that expanded notion has caught on here in the twenty-first century. The broader view is that each of us is born with a gift; that is to say, a set of talents, aptitudes, and inclinations that equip us as individuals to do something special. That something special may very well never lead to fame or notoriety, but we each have a purpose in life that involves making a contribution to the greater good that no one else can do in quite the same way we do.

We don't have to look far nowadays to find this kind of language about finding a purposeful life. And that's good news. Cayce's work is not alone in having spurred this kind of thinking, but it certainly played an invaluable role. And the expansion has reached not only into mainstream books, articles, and television programs. There is even an expanded interest in these kinds of themes in social science research. The topic here is meaning—not so much "What is the meaning of life?" because that's a philosophical and religious question; instead, there's growing interest in social science research about what makes life meaningful and how people find and pursue meaning, especially through their work.

To illustrate this growing interest, even among academics, here is one example. What are the implications of choosing a career that feels deeply meaningful and yet is likely to be undervalued in society, not pay very well, and have considerable workplace stress? Two researchers decided to investigate this riddle, and they chose zookeepers as the subjects of their study. Now at first most of us might be quick to dismiss such a study, simply because we don't have much interest in cleaning out monkey cages or lugging around huge crates of food for a hippo. However, this social science investigation does have relevance for any of us inclined toward a career in teaching, nursing, social work, and a whole host of other fields that involve care for others. In their 2009 peer-review journal article, titled "The Call of the Wild: Zookeepers, Callings, and the Double-edged Sword of Deeply Meaningful Work," researchers J. Stuart Bunderson and Jeffery A. Thompson describe an aspect of the human spirit that compels people to sacrifice pay, personal time, and comfort in service to work that they feel they were born to do. And as we see from the Cayce archives, his spiritual advice to many individuals was to listen for and follow just that sort of calling to meaningful work.

But evidence that discovering your soul's purpose is making it into a broader conversation isn't the only factor for the revision of this book. There is a deeper and more personal reason that answers the question "Why a new edition?" That answer is simply that I have been reinspired about how vital it is for people to hear their calling and fulfill the mission for which they were born. That reinspiration has come from working with and being around emerging adults every day at my job teaching at a large public university. The sincerity and depth of inquiry that I see in my students has once again made me aware of just how important this material really is. Perhaps some of this renewal of my own vision comes from the fact that my twenty- to twenty-two-year-old students are at just the same age as I was for my own intense search to discover my mission. In fact, I like to think there is a sort of positive karma in my being able to give back to people in this age group, because I was so profoundly helped by mentors and teachers at that period in my own journey.

AND MY WIFE, Mary Elizabeth Lynch, and I work increasingly with this age group through a nonprofit educational organization we cofounded in 2000, the Personal Transformation and Courage Institute (PTCI). When we have these emerging adults in our small-group course intensives, they show a willingness to courageously look at their lives and a deep longing to connect with their ideals and their talents so that they can fulfill their highest potential. With a wisdom often beyond their years, they inspire everyone in the group— so much so that Mary Elizabeth and I want to shift PTCI's outreach to focus more on emerging adults and helping them find their soul purpose.

And yet, the reinspiration is more than just being reminded of my own emerging adulthood several decades ago. It also has something to do with what's going on in today's world—something that young adults may be more attuned to than those who are older and more used to seeing things in a certain way. And so, in my everyday work life now, I go to class and we talk about mindfulness, and practices to support well-being, and the ways to express meaning in one's life in such a way that *other people are uplifted* by one's own way of being in the world. Young adults think deeply about these matters. Sure, they are worried about how they will ever pay off student loans, and they wonder how they will find a job when they graduate. But each one also intuitively senses that he or she is meant to do something significant in life. Each one feels a prompt or an intimation that his or her own contribution can be pivotal.

To a large extent the world hangs in the balance now. Human divisiveness and climate change are twin threats that have the potential to be as earthshaking and catastrophic as anything Cayce described in earth-change prophecies—predictions that seem to have never come true. But the scary truth of the matter is that things in the world cannot continue along the track they have been on. Surely some big changes are afoot. And if we are to find a graceful way to make it to a new world order—a new way of living together on and with the earth—then we need thousands, even millions of people to wake up to their callings. The emerging adults in my university classroom are a reminder and a reinspiration about just how important discovering your soul's purpose really is. But it's not just this generation. It's all of us.

Mark Thurston
December 2016
Fairfax, Virginia

The reason why we are disenchanted with ourselves is because we entertain in the depths of our psyche a kind of vision—an anticipated vision of what we could be if we would be what we might be.

Sufi master Pir Vilayat Khan, in a lecture,
October 15, 1983

In my own notes, I had at first labeled this defense [the "Jonah Complex"], "the fear of one's own greatness" or "the evasion of one's destiny" or "the running away from one's own best talent." . . . It is certainly possible for most of us to be greater than we are in actuality. We all have unused potentialities or not fully developed ones. It is certainly true that many of us evade our constitutionally suggested vocations . . . So often we run away from the responsibilities dictated (or rather suggested) by nature, by fate, even sometimes by accident, just as Jonah tried in vain to run away from his fate.

Excerpt from
The Farther Reaches of Human Nature,
by Abraham Maslow

All esotericism teaches that in order to go up, you have to go down, and no one understands what this means: to get more you must go down, and to get less you go in the same way as you always go—your Being transmits your life. If you have nothing at present that satisfies you completely, it is because of the state of your Being, and you will never get what you want as long as your Being is tuned in to that wavelength. You have to change yourself to get new influences, and changing yourself is always "getting rid of yourself." . . .

If you try to increase yourself as you are, you will only become worse than you are at present. The development of Real Will consists of feeling new influences.

Excerpt from
Psychological Commentaries on the Teachings of Gurdjieff
and Ouspensky, by Maurice Nicoll, M.D.

Introduction

You were born into this life for a purpose. "For, each soul enters with a mission" is the way that Edgar Cayce put it. "We all have a mission to perform" (3003-1). That purpose and living it are within your grasp; it is something that can be discovered and applied. Your soul's purpose gives your life a sense of fulfillment.

The title for this book has been carefully chosen. The initial word, *discovering*, is probably the most important one because your relationship to your life's mission is fundamentally an *ongoing* process of revelation. In other words, there is a dynamic, unfolding characteristic to the purposefulness of your life. Your soul's purpose is *not* something that is found once and for all and can then be "put in the trophy case" for all to admire. Instead, you should expect that throughout your life there will always be opportunities to discover more about your mission—some new characteristic of it or some new phase of it that is now ready to be lived.

This book is a collection of tools, techniques, and perspectives. It is a collage of ideas that need to be put into practice. It's all about application. If you try to engage the ideas of this book merely at a rational, analytical level, they are unlikely to lead to a discovery of your calling.

Instead, what is needed is an active application of the principles you will find here. If this book is to serve as a catalyst for your discovery of a life's mission, then you must proceed through these pages slowly—especially in the second third of the book, where you will encounter specific exercises in self-reflection and inner searching. This all takes some time to bear fruit.

Fundamentally, this book addresses a question that most of us ask periodically in our lives: Who am I to be? We wonder about what the future holds for us. We speculate about the possibility of something that might make our lives special, that would allow us to stand out in some unique way. It is not that we insist out of vanity on being better than everyone else. Instead, it is a natural and wonderful impetus from deep within the soul, from a place within us that knows the incredible splendor of individuality.

However, the question "Who am I to be?" is not one that can be quickly or easily answered. Instead, you must begin by asking, "Who am I *now*?" because your ignorance of your present self is to a large extent the primary barrier that keeps you from your destiny. In this sense, you must learn how to stop being the "old" (i.e., the familiar self-identity, the old ways of reacting to life, and so on) in order to clear the way for the emergence of "what is to be."

This principle is often presented in Edgar Cayce's philosophy. In speaking of mankind's natural desire to know about the future, he counsels us to remember that it's just as important to know from whence we have come—our roots, physically and psychologically—as it is to know where we are headed. Simply put: The adventure of this book will be as much about understanding the past and present as it will be about the future.

Elements of Wisdom as We Start the Journey

The theme of finding one's deepest calling is an ancient line of inquiry. People for millennia have asked themselves about the purposefulness of life. The three quotations that are found at the beginning of this introduction are modern pieces of wisdom about this universal sense of possibility and fulfillment.

The first passage is from a Sufi master, and it addresses the feeling that we all get from time to time. For some people that feeling becomes nearly constant—a restless disenchantment with oneself. That feeling is, in essence, the shadow side of one's inner vision of potential and possibilities. We sense that there is something more that we could be. That "something" is deeply related to one's calling—one's soul purpose. Once we intuit that it's there, residing within us, then we can never quite be satisfied with ourselves or our lives until we meet it and claim it.

The second passage also refers to what we might consider the shadow side of a calling. We tend to step back when our deepest purpose calls to us. We're not sure we're really up for it. We might reason that maybe someone else is really meant to fulfill what we feel called to do, just like Jonah in the biblical story. He was called by God to go and warn the people of Nineveh that destruction would befall them if they did not change their way of living (Jonah 1:1–2). But he ran away from the call, only eventually to be swallowed by a whale when he was thrown overboard from the ship in which he was fleeing. And haven't we all experienced to some degree what psychologist Abraham Maslow calls the "Jonah complex"— our avoidance of what a soul purpose might require of us?

The final opening quote is a bit more complex, and it comes from the writings of Dr. Maurice Nicoll, a psychiatrist and the author of many books about transformational psychology. This passage suggests that there is a deeper layer to who we really are, what might be called one's Being. However, most of our daily life proceeds from one's more ordinary personality self, "yourself as you are." And if we aspire to rise to the higher calling that comes from Being, paradoxically we have to go *down* before we can go *up*. It's a bit like the old adage that things have to get worse before they can get better. But isn't that often our experience with health and healing? An effective remedy may at first aggravate matters. To get more, you must go down. And that takes courage and faith because we prefer to get quick results from any self-improvement endeavor, especially something like finding one's soul purpose. Nicoll is simply warning us as we start on this kind of work: it's hard work and sometimes a bit disturbing to get to know ourselves more deeply.

The Cayce Life Readings

Between 1923 and 1944, Cayce gave more than nineteen hundred readings in which he tried to help people see their life's purpose. These came to be called the "life readings," and they form the basis of this book. Why was this type of reading so popular? Was it mere curiosity? Did people simply like to hear about themselves? Was it a fascination with reincarnation, which was a feature of nearly all the readings that fall into this category? No doubt all of these factors played a role.

But there is a deeper reason why the life readings were so important and so frequently requested. Something in all of us is hungry for a sense of meaning. As human beings we require some purpose for being. For thousands of years that innate impulse has generated the great philosophies of life and the religions of the world. People have tried to define the purpose of life on a cosmic scale and to answer the most fundamental riddles of human existence: How did we get here? Why does there seem to be injustice in the world? Do we survive physical death? Cayce's life readings offered answers to universal questions like these, but they did something more. They spoke to the individual about his or her own life. The life readings showed men and women how profound meaning and purpose can be discovered in the midst of mundane affairs. Cayce went so far as to suggest that it is within the ordinary aspects of life that something extraordinary can happen. In other words, making life great does not necessarily mean doing "great things" in the eyes of mainstream society. For example, something remarkable stands out about those few individuals who received praise in their life readings from Cayce's clairvoyant source—praise that stated they were on track with their real purposes in life. Most often they were plain, common people who were quietly fulfilling their potential for service and creativity.

Who Looks for a Purpose in Life?

What sorts of people came to Edgar Cayce asking for help in finding the purpose of life? In fact, they came from all walks of life, but they probably had in common one or more of these three characteristics:

1. Pain. This hurt is not the sort that stimulates a request for a physical health reading. Instead it's a woundedness that comes from deep within the soul—pain resulting from being unfulfilled and from knowing that things are not quite right.

It's a fact of human nature that we usually don't change unless we are hurting. Pain prods us toward growth. To see and understand this does not glorify pain or wish it upon us. But it reminds us of the significance of this kind of hurting. It is not something to be ignored or covered up. Rather, it is a longing for deeper meaning to our lives.

2. Dissatisfaction. Even when many things in life are going well, it's still possible to feel discontented. But this is not the petty, spoiled displeasure that always wants more of what the world has to offer. That sort of complaining attitude isn't likely to start someone on the search for a spiritual purpose. Instead, one experiences a paradox: feeling grateful for all the good in his or her life, but at the same time feeling dissatisfied, knowing that there must be something more. That "something more" is not a better paying job, or greater prestige at work, or more influence in the community. It is a new sense of meaning.

3. Restlessness with being comfortable. This characteristic may sound strange. After all, isn't comfort the thing we all look for? Isn't comfort the very ideal we strive for in a stressful world? Perhaps not, because after a while mere comfort becomes boring. Something in the human spirit eventually comes forth, ready for adventure and the next challenge. Something in all of us wants to wrestle with tension. That means grappling and struggling, not with the all-too-familiar hassles of daily living, but instead with this creative tension that resides in the soul: who we are now compared to who we have the potential to be.

Most likely the people who sought life readings from Cayce exhibited one or more of those characteristics. And it is likely that anyone who picks up this book also exhibits those characteristics. Therefore we might ask ourselves, "What inner quality is revealed by someone searching for the deepest purpose of life?" The answer probably is pain within the soul, dissatisfaction with the traditional values of the world, or a restlessness with the familiar, comfortable situation.

If you experience one or more of these characteristics, how

can Edgar Cayce help you? He has been dead for many decades, so you cannot get a life reading from him today. Other clairvoyants offer life readings, but are they accurate and reliable? Whether or not you choose to experiment with a modern-day psychic, the Cayce readings can play a key role in your search for your purpose in life. Even though these readings contain information given to other people, they can be of great assistance to you. How is that possible?

An analogy can be drawn with the physical health readings Cayce gave. For example, forty different people received psychic information from him about their psoriasis. All of them lived in the 1920s, 1930s, and 1940s. How could someone with psoriasis, living eighty or more years later, derive any help from those readings? Surprisingly, many have. A careful study shows some of the information was quite individual and no doubt relevant only to the person given the reading. However, when these readings are compared, we see recurrent themes. Cayce described distinct patterns concerning the origins of psoriasis and recommended similar treatments. In recent years, people have worked with these repeated themes; many have obtained relief from this skin condition.

The same principle can be used with the life readings. Patterns can be found in the way Cayce counseled people to find their highest purpose in life. Consistency is found in this material in both its theory concerning the meaning of life and the techniques given for finding one's own specific purpose. Even though a seeker today cannot get a personalized Cayce life reading, it is still possible to work with his approach. And just as there are many reports of success from people who apply recurrent patterns in the health readings, so too are there many reports from people who have found their own purpose in life from following the Cayce life readings.

This book describes how to use a strategy found again and again in those life readings. It draws upon the best insights and methods from information Cayce gave to hundreds of people much like you. This book presents those insights and methods along with other spiritual teachings, and shows you how to find your own purpose and fulfill your destiny in life. By applying these ideas you will have a practical program for bringing greater meaning into your life. It's an adventure in self-discovery and a journey to become the person you were born to be. If you will follow the steps described in this book, you will create for yourself something every bit as valuable as a personalized Cayce life reading!

Hindrances to Finding Your Purpose

This exciting journey to fulfillment is not without obstacles and difficulty. As we already saw in Maurice Nicoll's passage about the need to go down before we can go up, a certain measure of faith, courage, and resilience is needed for this kind of adventure. But if you know what these points of resistance are likely to be, then you will be better equipped to deal with them when they arise.

What are some of those impediments? Many are related to the values and methods of our society. For all the talk of personal freedom and individuality, we do not live in a culture that truly honors the uniqueness of each soul. The problem begins early in life: Childhood education is based largely on "norms" or baseline averages, to which the child is pushed to conform.

Whether you remember it or not, chances are much of your unique way of learning and creating was covered up early in life and replaced by the way teachers wanted for you. Not that it was done with any evil intention, but a barrier was possibly created within you anyway. No doubt you learned considerable amounts of useful information in school. The point here is not that school is wrong. But for many of us—likely most of us—a certain portion of our own, individual flair for living was stifled by our childhood education.

Like all barriers and obstacles, any misdirected methods of childhood education can be overcome. It is always possible to reclaim the ingredients of your soul that are needed in order to fulfill your purpose in life. Some of us just have to work a little harder than others to recover what has been lost or forgotten.

A second hurdle we face by living in modern society is mechanization. Admittedly we all benefit from modern technology, which gives us things that we would find hard to live without. And successfully living our spiritual purpose hardly requires returning to the lifestyle of the eighteenth century. Nevertheless, subtle and detrimental effects within the human soul are produced by the process of mechanization. What happens with each new breakthrough yielding yet another laborsaving machine? Quite easily we can lose touch with our human capacity to get things done. Weakened even more is a healthy and indispensable aspect of the soul: the human will.

The will is that elusive and uniquely human gift that allows us to be creative. Furthermore, it empowers us to get things done in life—to go beyond just dreaming about projects and high purposes. It is the will that permits us to express what we are called to do.

We should look carefully at what happens to our will forces in an age of mechanization—of televisions, iPads, and gaming systems that diminish the need for our own creative imagination, of iPods and Internet streaming music that trivialize the need to make music for ourselves.

Of course neither Cayce nor the other sources for this book say that we should abandon the usefulness of machines. Be assured that you can work with the practical steps outlined here without feeling obligated to give away your television, tablet computer, or gaming system, sell off your wireless speakers, or throw away your smartphone. But also, be aware of just how important it is to have a healthy will that has not slipped into laziness because of laborsaving machines. In order to be successful in living your highest purpose, you will need to be creative, imaginative, and active in the world. Make sure that the products of a mechanized age are your servants and not the other way around.

Closely related to the problem of mechanization is a third impediment to finding and living your purpose in life. Not everyone faces this hindrance, but many people are in jobs that are highly specialized and filled with mind-numbing routine. Machines don't object to repetitive tasks; that's what they are best at. But people aren't meant to be mechanical. Something in us all wants to be creative and not stuck in a rut. This holds true for every part of living, but it is especially encountered as a problem in our occupations.

If you find yourself in a job that is routinized and boring, this book may or may not lead you to leave that job for another occupation. For practical reasons it could be necessary to stay in that job for a while. But there is one thing you can be especially careful about: Try to avoid letting the sense of automatic, habitual living from your workplace spill over into the other parts of your life. Keep a fresh, creative spontaneity alive in your relationships, your home life, and your free time alone.

There is a fourth likely obstacle in the journey to becoming the person you were born to be. It is one of the hallmarks of the modern age: Almost everyone is plagued with a feeling of constant busyness. Is your life cluttered with far too much to do? Do you frequently feel the strain of too many demands? It may come in the form of friends for whom you never seem to have time, or a boss who wants results far quicker than they can be accomplished with quality. Or you may feel this constant busyness as little tugs at your conscience, reminding you that too many things are being left unfinished: a disorganized closet or garage, a Sunday newspaper left unread, an e-mail that remains unanswered for weeks.

What is the solution? Something in you may say the answer couldn't depend on *further* commitments. Your lists are already long enough, and they hardly have room for other items such as "purpose" in life. This sense of busyness can easily keep you from looking for a deeper meaning to your existence. You may feel too pressed for time and too fatigued from it all.

And yet the only way out of this common bottleneck is to set new priorities. Only by getting a fresh vision of the meaning of your life can you free yourself from the tyranny of your lists and never-ending obligations. The sole method for freeing up your time and creative energy is to put your whole life in a new perspective—to see things with a different set of criteria.

What are you likely to find when you start on this kind of adventure? What insights are bound to come when you start discovering your unique purpose in life? Much of what clutters and fills up your day has little or nothing to do with your real purpose in life. What a revelation!

PART I

The Four-Step Pattern

Let each individual know that it came into life with a purpose from God. Let each individual know that it is as a harp upon which the breath of God would play. While all may not be as prophets or as preachers, neither may all stand in the halls of learning as directors of men, know that you each have your part to do. (281-60)

PART I OF this book provides the framework for seeking and trying to define a mission in life. These opening four chapters present the theory and the philosophy from the Cayce material, culminating in an exercise to craft a personal mission statement. Then in part II we begin the work of personal application to see how that soul purpose can be lived.

The structure of part I is based on the idea that personal transformation unfolds in an orderly way. We're all familiar with the axiom "First things first." Simply stated, it means that there is an orderly and necessary sequence to how things unfold. When we are impatient or when we want to do things our own way, we may find ourselves frustrated by this principle. But if we are wise, then we'll appreciate that the "orderliness of unfoldment" exists as a universal law that supports us and makes it easier for us to find our way.

Think about this analogy from mathematics: When you begin to learn algebra, you cannot just jump in and start solving complex algebraic equations. First, as a preschooler, you learned your numbers; then, as a grade-schooler, you learned to add, subtract, multiply, and divide. Each step in your learning built upon the previous one. There was an orderly unfoldment of your mathematical understanding that eventually prepared you to start dealing with more complex problems.

Many traditions of transformational psychology articulate examples of these sequences of unfoldment. One example comes from the teaching of G. I. Gurdjieff and P. D. Ouspensky. (Ouspensky, a Russian teacher of consciousness transformation, was, in fact, one of the few writers explicitly recommended in the Cayce readings.) These men were contemporaries of Cayce, all born in the 1870s, and even though their work was done in different places in the world, there are many parallels in their teachings. In chapter 2 we'll be exploring in more depth some of the principles of personal transformation that come from Gurdjieff and Ouspensky and see how closely they resemble the philosophy of Cayce.

These two teachers proposed the Law of the Octave, which suggests that the seven musical notes that repeat themselves as an octave on a keyboard (i.e., do-re-mi-fa-so-la-ti) exhibit a powerful analogy for how human consciousness progresses through reliable stages as it unfolds. The first note, do, corresponds to giving valuation to something in our lives, such as placing a high priority on teachings about spiritual develop-

ment. This kind of valuation is as much an emotional investment as it is a rational decision that something is important
to us. There needs to be real *feeling* to giving something central value in one's life.

Re corresponds to the application of teachings—not just
valuing them and studying them, but actually starting to act
on them. This is also a key tenet in the Cayce material, as he
asserts that it's only in the application of a principle that we
can truly understand it.

Mi corresponds to what inevitably arises when we start
trying to apply principles of personal transformation: We encounter resistance from within ourselves, an internal push-
back that resists change. Everyone knows this stage from
personal experience. We don't change easily. We don't move
to a higher understanding of life easily. There is always resistance, and we must be able to see that the obstacles are ultimately internal ones.

This Law of the Octave goes on to say that we reach a
critical juncture when trying to reach the fourth stage of orderly unfoldment, and we're invited to consider that there is
no black key on the piano keyboard between the notes mi
and fa. This is the "missing semitone," and what's required
now is an *internal force* that lifts our consciousness to fa—a
"shock" that comes from a meditation-like shift to remember
one's true self, one's spiritual essence or individuality. Only
then, at this fourth stage of the sequence, does something
entirely new begin to emerge from the deepest being of oneself. In fact, this movement to fa is what's required of us to
find and to live our soul purpose.

So, what is the equivalent teaching in the Cayce material? Where in the Cayce readings do we see something akin to Gurdjieff and Ouspensky's Law of the Octave? Perhaps it is the sequence outlined in *A Search for God*—a progression of lessons that can lead to personal transformation and an awakening to our true calling in life. Of course, Cayce's growth sequence has many more steps than the repeating seven-step sequence that we find in a musical octave. But if we focus on the first four steps of *A Search for God*, we will find something equally insightful and of practical value as we assess our own spiritual growth and development. Consider how this might provide a template for our journey to discover a personal mission. The sequence of Cooperation, Know Thyself, What Is My Ideal? and Faith collectively creates a pattern to follow in finding one's calling.

Cooperation is first because no further development is possible unless we learn how to act in harmony with God, ourselves, and others. What's more, since the *A Search for God* program was especially designed for group study, cooperation was a prerequisite just for the group to function. But it means more than simply getting along with other people. It ultimately leads to *being able to love and appreciate (and cooperate with) all the parts of oneself.* Cooperation is going to be a starting point as chapter 1—just as the Law of the Octave begins with the note do.

Self-knowledge comes second in the *A Search for God* sequence. We're reminded of the admonition of the Delphic oracle in ancient Greece: Know thyself. Anything else we try to do on the spiritual path rests on shaky ground unless we have some beginnings of authentic self-awareness with which to proceed. Total self-realization isn't demanded at this early step—simply an emerging understanding of who we really are. An initial insight about one's true nature is like a seed that will sprout, grow, blossom, and give fruit as the other steps of the program are applied. Being able to see and know oneself is the vital second step in finding one's soul calling, and that will be our focus for chapter 2.

Once we start to have some revelations about our true character and individuality, then we can effectively choose *values, goals, and ideals* that will lead to living our soul purpose. Cayce's *A Search for God* readings on this third step warned how easily we can go wrong. Even with the best of intentions, it's easy to set ideals that are based on misperceptions of ourselves. For example, we can mistake an ordinary part of the personality for the Higher Self. The side of us that is nice or polite or friendly is not necessarily the deepest spiritual identity. Today's world is full of spiritual novices who are quick to claim, "I am God," but are they actually in touch with such a depth of reality, or have they settled for an appealing slogan that is a shortcut? Only when we have first made some progress in self-study can we begin to see with any clarity which goals and aims are truly worth shooting for. Otherwise, we slip into self-delusion that merely reinforces and deepens our misunderstanding of life. And so, the central theme for chapter 3 is this quest to identify core values and to set a personal spiritual ideal.

And then the fourth step is *faith*. In the Cayce philosophy this means *the actual experience of unseen reality*. It's not just having really strong beliefs, as important as that may be. Faith is a matter of having *direct encounters* with the realm of the soul. Here is where we open ourselves to have an experience of a calling from deep within—the invitation to see and embrace a soul purpose. That will be the focus of chapter 4. And if we try to jump right to hearing the call without having first done the work of steps one through three, then it's not going to work for us, any more than we can start our mathematical training by trying to solve tough algebra problems.

Keeping in mind this fourfold architecture for part I, let's go ahead and get started with our exploration of the cooperative spirit that makes the journey possible.

CHAPTER I

Cooperation, Meaning, and Mission

Not my will but Thine, O Lord, be done in me and through me. Let me ever be a channel of blessings, today, now, to those that I contact in every way. Let my going in, my coming out be in accord with that Thou would have me do, and as the call comes, "Here am I, send me, use me." (262-3)

THIS PRAYERFUL AFFIRMATION provides a perfect foundation for understanding Cayce's approach to finding one's personal mission. It addresses free will, the importance of making a contribution to the well-being of others, and the sense of a call to a higher purpose. Cayce offered these words as a focal point for meditation, linked to the first step in the *A Search for God* soul-growth sequence.

In a sense, this affirmation about cooperation is a distillation of this entire book and the systematic steps to discover your soul's purpose. It invites you to understand the word *cooperation* in a distinctly spiritual way—something that hinges on right use of your free will. The affirmation invites you to consider how your own happiness and fulfillment are linked to the well-being of others. And the affirmation underscores how deep cooperation depends upon having an orientation of *willingness* in your life—willingness to respond to life as an interconnected whole with which you can cooperate.

Cooperation means more, though, than just being open to connections to something bigger than yourself. It is also about cooperating with *yourself*, as strange as that may sound. Consider for a moment how we often don't cooperate with ourselves. Most fundamentally, that noncooperative spirit is expressed as self-judgment and self-criticism. We are usually our own worst critic! And it's quite revolutionary to turn this tendency around and practice profound self-acceptance. Ultimately this first step—the shift to self-cooperation and healthy self-love—makes it possible for us to go on a search for meaning and purpose.

What does it feel like to practice self-acceptance? That kind of internal cooperation might feel spacious. We give ourselves the gift of having room to breathe, so to speak. Most of the time, our self-judgment and voices of self-criticism crowd in on us, leaving us feeling trapped and disappointed in life. On the other hand, when we can love ourselves and give ourselves the benefit of the doubt, that gentleness creates a whole new environment in which we can start to flourish. Just being kind to ourselves, just having deep respect for ourselves—these expressions of self-cooperation really are step number one in trying to find the soul's calling. Self-cooperation sets the stage for us to be able to address the deepest need of the soul: the need for meaning.

Meaning and the Soul

What do we need to survive? The list of obvious answers includes air, food, and shelter. We can never deny the inescapable fact that we have physical bodies, and survival depends on meeting their basic requirements.

However, something else distinguishes us from other creatures who have physical needs. That extra ingredient is an individual soul, and like the physical body, it must be nurtured to survive. The human soul may be invisible to scientific instruments, but each of us experiences its reality daily. Each time we say "I" to ourselves, we feel the presence of the soul. Every instance of aspiration, enthusiasm, or free will is an expression of our own soul nature. And yet, as real and immediate as the soul may be, it still needs nourishment and sustenance each day.

What is the air, food, and shelter of the soul? What keeps it alive and active? The answer is *meaning*. The human soul grows and develops as it can make sense of life and set aspirations for the future.

The Edgar Cayce readings returned to this point time and again as they advised people how to find happiness. The hundreds of people who received his guidance were given a promise that *everything* about life is meaningful. That promise extends to each of us. We are assured there is a rhyme and a reason to what happens to us.

When we stop to think about it, this is an amazing promise. So much goes on in our world that seems senseless. It's easy to be cynical because every day we are likely to learn about or directly encounter cruelty, dishonesty, and injustice. Not only do things often appear to be unfair, it's easy to conclude that nothing is really in charge, that life is random and pointless.

In almost every century of human history, some individuals have made a special effort to point out the signs of despair and chaos. They voice an ancient cry of hopelessness. However, other people have been able to look at the same events and conditions with a different perspective. They have spoken and written about the meaning of life. They have seen how both pleasant and unpleasant experiences are purposeful.

If we look at the twentieth century as an example—the century in which Edgar Cayce did his work—we can see both sides of the debate. For example, the first fifty years saw great tragedies and disasters, including two world wars and a global economic depression. There were ample reasons to despair. Yet during those same fifty years, there lived pioneers of a renewed sense of meaning for our own postindustrial society. Since then we have built on the creativity of these key individuals. Let's look briefly at three of them—Carl Jung, Edgar Cayce, and Viktor Frankl—and the new ideas they presented about the meaning of life.

Carl Jung and the Process of Individuation

Carl Jung was the founder of analytical psychology. A contemporary of Cayce, he was born in 1875, just two years before the clairvoyant whose work parallels his so closely. The son of a Swiss clergyman, Jung trained as a psychiatrist.

In his early professional years he was a supporter and protégé of Sigmund Freud. A rift, however, developed between the two, primarily over the question of the unconscious mind. Freud viewed the hidden side of the psyche as driven by repressed sexuality. And while Jung did not deny the findings of his teacher, colleague, and friend, he felt that something more lay within the unconscious aspect of every person. Research with his patients and the study of his own dreams convinced him that the unconscious also contains innate impulses toward wholeness and mental health.

Out of Jung's long career as a psychiatrist, teacher, and writer developed a psychology of the human soul. Rather than seeing spirituality and religion as an evasion of mental health, he recognized the need for psychiatry and faith to find a common ground. For him the answer lay in a synthesis of Eastern and Western religious traditions. He recognized that each of these two great streams of spirituality had something vital to offer humanity in its search for meaning.

Much of the history of the Western hemisphere has emphasized our physical existence as individual beings and the historical fact of the Christ. Jung felt that Christians are most likely to look outside themselves for a divine presence who can bestow grace. In contrast, the East has featured universality, timelessness, and the inner life. Jung put it this way: "The Oriental knows that redemption depends on the work he does on himself. The Tao grows out of the individual."*

What is this mysterious Tao? Some have translated it as

---

* Carl Jung, "Commentary on the Secret of the Golden Flower" in *The Collected Works of C. G. Jung*, volume 13 (New York: Bollingen Foundation, 1960), p. 53.

God or Providence. However, Jung believed that the best interpretation is *meaning*. In other words, those of us who live in the West must learn to appreciate that meaning grows out of our own individuality and the work that we do within ourselves. For Jung there was a great disadvantage in the Western approach to imitate Christ. Even though the Christ may have "embodied the deepest meaning of life [nevertheless] . . . we forget to make real our own deepest meaning."* We can easily forget the task of self-realization. In fact it's often convenient to avoid what would be most meaningful to us as individuals and to take the path of least resistance. Jung imagines that if Jesus had evaded self-realization, he would have become a respectable carpenter.

One of Jung's books, a collection of essays on the quest for meaning in life, is appropriately titled *Modern Man in Search of a Soul*. He came to believe that the deepest part of the mind is transpersonal—extending beyond the bounds of one individual. This level of the "collective unconscious" is a common trait of all humanity. Within these deep strata of the mind are universal patterns that can shape and direct the development of our lives. Jung called them "archetypes," the most important of which is the Self.

What is this curious component called the Self? What role does it play in the search for a meaningful life? According to Jung, this universal pattern of wholeness, the Self, lives within each of us. We might be tempted to say that it is sleeping

---

* Ibid.

inside us, but perhaps it is *we* who are asleep in our daily, familiar consciousness!

Even though the Self is universal, it is expressed within every one of us in a different way. Each soul has its own special potential and gifts. However, the discovery process takes considerable time and allows no shortcuts. By working diligently throughout our lives, we can respond to and receive this inner wholeness into our conscious awareness. For Jung this is the essential purpose and meaning of life: to fulfill the potential of our own authentic being.

Even though all of this may sound vague, one of Jung's greatest contributions was to provide a map of the journey to wholeness. He called this adventure the process of *individuation*. It is a path to self-realization and meaning that is available to everyone, but few people walk it to the end.

Generally speaking the process of individuation takes place over two phases of life that are divided at roughly age forty. The so-called midlife crisis marks the opportunity to move into the second and more difficult aspect of individuation, and most people get bogged down or diverted at this point. Success in phase two requires something in addition to courage and wisdom. During the years preceding forty, there must have also been the development of a healthy persona.

In Jungian terms the persona is a mask, or a series of masks, we wear in life. It is a way of adapting to the demands of society. No doubt this facade can become dishonest and inauthentic, but Jung proposed that it's possible to develop a healthy persona. It is a marvelous accomplishment to move through the challenges we face between puberty and age forty and come out with a sound, balanced self-image. It means steering a course between many conflicting demands. This period of approximately twenty-five years is full of conflicting life choices: freedom versus commitment, planning versus spontaneity, privacy versus intimacy, just to name a few. According to Jung, it's probably not best to strive for wholeness during this first phase of the individuation process. That important work comes in phase two. Instead the young adult develops a healthy persona by temporarily focusing on just a few qualities, picking one side of a pair of opposites over the other side. During phase one we adopt an orientation toward life—choosing between what he called introversion and extroversion. And we begin to strengthen and sharpen certain talents and skills, even if it means that other sides of ourselves must be temporarily ignored. The result can be a reasonably healthy, productive individual who has positive ego strength and is prepared for the more difficult tasks that come after age forty.

During the second phase of life we have the chance to discover a deeper and more personal meaning to life. This is the time in which we strive for wholeness and begin to complement our obvious talents and strengths with their forgotten opposites. The accomplished organizer discovers a richer meaning to life by experiencing spontaneity. The emotional, feeling-oriented person explores the kind of meaning that comes from logic and analysis.

How prepared are we for this difficult venture? How many

people know how to find their personal meaning in life after this turning point around age forty? Jung wrote: "Wholly unprepared, they embark upon the second half of life. Or are there perhaps colleges for forty-year-olds which prepare them for their coming life and its demands as the ordinary colleges introduce our young people to a knowledge of the world? No, thoroughly unprepared we take the step into the afternoon of life."*

Jung's life work was to create a map to guide modern men and women through those uncharted waters. His spiritual psychology largely concerns the process of individuation. His system teaches how to find one's personal meaning in life. That task of individuation has two steps to be taken after age forty. First we must become more and more aware of those sides of ourselves that have been ignored. It requires courage to look at parts of the soul that we have disregarded for many years. However scary it may be, those hidden aspects have a great gift to offer.

The second step of individuation is the quest for wholeness. In step one we recognize the forgotten parts of ourselves; in step two we embrace them and find a place for them. They will enrich us and bring us to new revelations about the meaning of life. That meaning comes from the realization of uniqueness and individuality. This is the highest goal in Jungian psychology: the development and awakening of one's own distinctive, special personhood.

---

* Carl Jung, "The Stages of Life" in *The Collected Works of C. G. Jung*, volume 8 (New York: Bollingen Foundation, 1960), pp. 398–99.

Edgar Cayce and the Mission in Life

As great and helpful as Jungian contributions undoubtedly are, the ideas and philosophy of the Cayce readings add extra dimensions. Remember, these two great men worked during the same years, an ocean apart and apparently unaware of each other. Both dedicated their lives to helping people find meaning and purpose. Both understood the significance of the spiritual side of humanity. How, then, can their contributions be merged to give us the clearest and most valuable guidance for finding our own meaning in life?

No evidence suggests that Cayce was consciously aware of Jung's ideas. Nevertheless, Jung's own model of the collective unconscious implies that the clairvoyant Cayce might have drawn from the same source as Jung's inspiration.

Certain marked differences in the lives of these two men make it all the more astonishing that their philosophies of life contain so many close parallels. Where Jung completed rigorous academic programs, including a medical degree, Cayce's formal education only went as far as eighth grade. He was largely a self-taught man. Where Jung's colleagues and associates were among the most influential in Europe, Cayce's friends and supporters were most frequently common folk. And yet both of them made use of their remarkable talents to help other people find meaning in life. Their systems of thought and insights about human nature complement each other. Let's examine some of the ways that Cayce's readings added ingredients that enrich Jung's concept of personal individuation.

The Cayce readings agreed that each soul should strive for self-realization, but didn't give as many details as did Jung about the inner map of that journey. The readings defined particular spiritual disciplines that are crucial—prayer, meditation, dream study, and techniques to enrich physical health—but we don't find in the Cayce readings as many in-depth case studies of self-realization as we do in the body of Jung's published writings.

However, the Cayce readings added a special flavor to the theory of individuation. They described how each soul is born with a unique mission in life—every one of us is specially equipped with talents and abilities that give us the potential to make a needed contribution to the world. In other words, individuation is not the goal in itself. It prepares us for the task of living a specific mission for which we as souls came into this world. One familiar adage from the readings told many people, "Be not only good but be good for something!" (2868-2). Quite easily we can restate this principle: "Don't be just self-realized—be self-realized *for* something."

What did the Cayce readings mean by a "mission"? Various synonyms were used from time to time. Sometimes it was called the person's purpose in life. In other cases it was referred to as a personal destiny. In this sense the word *destiny* did not indicate a fate that was unavoidable, but rather an optimal potential for which the soul had all the necessary elements. Wise choices and determination are needed for anyone to successfully achieve his or her destiny.

We might just as readily think of the mission as the fulfillment of one's gift. Do you imagine yourself to be gifted? If you are like most people, you are probably reluctant to assume this label. Great musicians, athletes, and painters are gifted. And a very small minority of children may qualify for the gifted program at their schools. However, the Cayce readings proposed that you and everyone you know are gifted in a particular way. Each individual has a gift—a kind of sensitivity or talent. The very essence of a soul's mission is to discover that gift and then present it to the world.

Another synonym for *mission* is *calling*. In fact the Latin root of the word *vocation* means "to call." A career in religion is one of the few areas where people still speak directly of this deepest sense of vocation. For example, someone might say that he or she is called to the ministry or a religious order. Most often the term *vocation* is used interchangeably with *occupation* and *profession*. Cayce urged us to think of our life journeys as true vocations. We are called to be something and to do something. That calling comes from God and our own most authentic selves.

Another way in which the Cayce readings added to Jung's notion of individuation concerns service. Studying Jung, one never gets the idea that the fully individuated person will necessarily feel compelled to reach out to others. In the Cayce readings the message is definite: Each soul has a mission that includes the dimension of service. Spiritual evolution for humanity is a collective proposition. One reading put it bluntly: "You'll not be in heaven if you're not leaning on the arm of someone you have helped" (3352-1).

This polarity is a key to Cayce's theory of the meaning of life: the inner work of self-realization on one side and compassionate service on the other. An aspect of your soul's mission is the inner discovery process of finding your genuine, spiritual identity. And equally important, your mission and calling is to share your gifts and talents with others so that they too can fulfill their purposes.

Another contemporary of Edgar Cayce's wrote eloquently about these same two ingredients of life's meaning: the inner search for a personal mission and our responsibilities of service. Let's consider the school of psychotherapy established by Viktor Frankl. Like Jungian psychology, Frankl's logotherapy provides another line of parallel study for understanding the Cayce readings.

Viktor Frankl and Logotherapy

The biography of Viktor Frankl is one of the most inspiring of the twentieth century. A successful and respected psychiatrist in Vienna, Frankl was thrown into a concentration camp by the Nazis during World War II. No one who has read his detailed and horrific account of life in Auschwitz and Dachau is likely to forget its impact. It was first published as *From Death-Camp to Existentialism* and then as part one of *Man's Search for Meaning*. During these years of dehumanizing imprisonment, Frankl made important discoveries about human nature and the essence of meaning itself. When the war ended and he gained his freedom, he began to incorporate his new understanding into the way he treated his patients. Out of this work came an entire system of psychiatry, which he called logotherapy.

Frankl's assumption was that each person lives in three spheres: physical, mental, and spiritual. It's the third sphere that makes us truly human. It's within the realm of the spiritual (as opposed to the religious) that we encounter our need for meaning. Commenting on the psychiatric approach of two colleagues, he admitted that we have a *will to pleasure* (that is, the Freudian position) and a *will to power* (the Adlerian position), but he proposed a third drive that is even more significant: the *will to meaning.* In other words, there is an innate human impulse to discover what is purposeful about life, and when that drive is thwarted, we are likely to become sick in some form. Frankl cited statistical research that concluded that as much as 20 percent of illness in the modern world is directly attributable to the patient's failure to find meaning in life. We might well imagine that this percentage has only gone up in the decades since!

It is within our power to be successful in this exploration. We are equipped with the tools to do the job. According to Frankl, three components are at the core of every human being. First is spirituality: Our very substance and soul nature contains profound meaning. Second is freedom: We are beings of free will who often try to avoid that freedom of choice. Yet in spite of hereditary or environmental obstacles, each of us ultimately makes the decisions that shape the quality of our lives. This point is vividly driven home by Frankl's stories of concentration camp inmates who maintained their sense of integrity and inner freedom in spite of the most horrible conditions. And third is responsibility—but responsibility to

whom? First, Frankl stated, to ourselves and our own conscience. But just as clearly, he believed we are responsible to
our Creator to make the best possible use of what we have
been given.

Meaning was so central to Frankl's therapeutic approach
that he chose the term *logotherapy*. For him *logos* signified the
spiritual element—that which is meaningful. However, his
system is not an easy one. It demands a fundamental change
in how we view life. He concluded that we must begin to
question ourselves in a new way. Here is his most fundamental and succinct statement about how we start to find meaning. (The reader should keep in mind that Frankl intended
his generic use of the word *man* to denote all people—men
and women.)

> I have said that *man should not ask what he may expect from
> life, but should rather understand that life expects something
> from him*. It may also be put this way: in the last resort man
> should not ask "What is the meaning of my life?" but should
> realize that he himself is being questioned. Life is putting
> its problems to him, and it is up to him to respond to these
> questions by being responsible; he can only answer to his
> life by answering *for his* life.*

This way of thinking may not have been popular in Frankl's
time, nor is it now. Something in us prefers to believe that life

---

* Viktor Frankl, *The Doctor and the Soul* (New York: Alfred A. Knopf, 1955), p. xiii.

owes us something. However, Frankl's teaching is essentially the message of love. We can expect to find fulfillment not so much from what we *get* but from what we *give*.

Perhaps it shouldn't be surprising that Frankl has been more or less forgotten by contemporary psychology and mainstream culture. It is more fashionable and marketable to talk about what seekers can get rather than what they need to give. In times that promise, "You can have it all!" not many people want to hear the quiet, intense voice of a psychiatrist who survived Nazi concentration camps. Something about Frankl's central idea is apt to make us nervous. We already feel pressured by expectations from children, spouses, bosses, and the government. Who wants to imagine that life itself expects things of us?

However, in a paradoxical way maybe Frankl (and Cayce, who expressed the same themes) had the solution to our restless search for meaning in life. By giving we receive. By gladly accepting more responsibility we feel greater power. By making honest commitments we experience inner freedom.

For Frankl all of this came down to a basic truth about each life: Everyone is called to be and to do something unique. This fundamental premise is not an invitation to a messianic complex. That special calling is not to straighten out other people or the world. However, it is a promise that each one of us really does count, and it suggests that something deep within us will always remain uneasy until we discover and live what we were born to do. In what was perhaps his most concise statement of this idea, Frankl wrote:

One should not search for an abstract meaning of life. Everyone has his own specific vocation or mission in life; everyone must carry out a concrete assignment that demands fulfillment. Therein he cannot be replaced, nor can his life be repeated. Thus, everyone's task is as unique as is his specific opportunity to implement it.*

The language and terminology may differ, but Jung, Cayce, and Frankl all presented a common message: We need to love and appreciate who we are as souls. We need to be willing to practice cooperation with ourselves *and* with something bigger than ourselves. Life is essentially meaningful for any individual who will make the effort to explore his or her unique abilities. We are similar enough that certain steps along that pathway are universal. Yet each of us is also distinct and special in what we have to offer the world. These three teachers masterfully pointed the way and helped thousands of people to fulfill their inner potential.

Getting Oriented in the Search for Meaning

Where do you start in finding your own mission? What is the first step in discovering your purpose in life? Because your mission is special and customized to fit you, it may sound like a lonesome journey, one that is hard to begin.

---

* Viktor Frankl, *Man's Search for Meaning* (New York: Washington Square Press, 1963), p. 172.

Take heart—you aren't alone. Even though your purpose in life is distinctive, many elements of your search are shared by everyone. Consider this analogy: The purpose of life is like a two-sided coin. One face of the coin is the same for everyone; the other is unique to each individual. On the one hand, every soul has the same purpose. Together we are on an adventure in spiritual development that is more or less identical for every soul. Humanity is evolving in consciousness, and the process has been going on for thousands of years. That immense stream of development includes you.

However, at the same time you find yourself in the world with particular opportunities and challenges. You are not merely a bit player in some cosmic drama. Your life matters, and it has its own distinctive meaning. It is both natural and fitting for you to feel the impulse to know and live your own calling.

The trick is to see how two sides of a coin work together. The two aspects, commonality and uniqueness, do not describe competing purposes; they are two facets of the same meaning for life. To state the issue in philosophical terms: Universality and individuality don't have to be contradictions; they can complement each other like positive and negative poles of a magnet.

Maybe this still sounds like an insolvable paradox. You may find yourself wondering, "Am I really free to create my own destiny, or am I just a little cog in some inevitable process for all humanity?" The answer is you don't have to choose one or the other. As a spiritual being you have the freedom to shape your future and give meaning to your life. And at the same time, your personal destiny is a part of a greater plan. A general outline for soul development guides you, but there is also room for individuality and creativity.

For another analogy, imagine a class of twenty-five art students taking a sculpture course. The general requirement for all students is a final project—some kind of original sculpture that represents what each student has learned during the semester. But even this universal rule leaves considerable room for individuality. One student may choose clay as a medium for her project; another student, wood. One student may sculpt a bust; another, an abstract object. All twenty-five students must exhibit the techniques that have been demonstrated by the studio teacher, and yet there is flexibility that allows individual differences to shine through.

For some people the word *universality* creates a problem. They confuse it with conformity. In so many ways modern society stifles creativity and originality by forcing people to accommodate themselves to a general pattern. We are expected to dress in certain ways, to eat particular kinds of food, to meet specific standards of success. It's no wonder that the spiritual core of who we are rebels against this kind of compliance. Conformity demands that we shed our distinctiveness and reduce ourselves to some least common denominator of human nature. In sharp contrast, universality invites us to reach more deeply into our unique selves and find the very best of who we are.

And so there is good reason to appreciate both sides of the coin in our search for meaning and purpose. We must recognize that personal meaning in life requires a context. Purpose does not live in a vacuum; it needs to be part of something larger. For this reason there was a pattern in the way the Cayce readings advised people about their unique missions. The theory of this clairvoyant counselor was that personal meaning lives within the framework of many additional factors. To really understand what you are called to be and to do in this lifetime, you are encouraged to see it in the context of three ingredients:

1. *Your mission for this lifetime has a background of many previous missions in many other lifetimes.* Cayce suggests that the soul reincarnates, coming into bodily expression with a specialized purpose each time. In some incarnations you have been successful in fulfilling your mission; in other lifetimes you have probably allowed yourself to be diverted from your real calling. And so, based on accomplishments and failures from the past, there is a context for your current mission. (Belief in reincarnation is *not* a requirement in order to work with Cayce's system for finding your purpose in life. For those readers who would like to study some ideas about this controversial theory, appendix II takes a look at its implications. However, the Cayce readings themselves told people to work with the idea only if the evidence made sense to them.)

2. *Your mission for this lifetime is part of a network of missions.* Family members, neighbors, professional colleagues, and friends have their own purposes in life. You are drawn together because of the way you can

help each other toward success. Your unique purpose exists in the context of your social setting. What you are called to be in life fits remarkably well with the purposes of other souls around you. Although it doesn't always work out in the optimal way, there is the potential for you to fulfill your mission so that it interweaves with those of key people in your life.

3. *Your mission for this lifetime has been chosen against the backdrop of God's plan for all souls.* There is a grand design for the evolution of human consciousness, and your soul has been a part of that blueprint for many ages. This is the truly universal context in which you can begin to see clearly the special meaning of your own life.

However, in order to appreciate the cosmic framework in which you and everyone else live, you must be willing to study and speculate about the most distant times in human history. Quite naturally you may puzzle, "Must I really be concerned with things from thousands of years ago if all I want to understand is my life right now?" Cayce's response to this sort of doubt was that yes, it is valuable. As he said in one reading, "There is as much reason to dwell upon the thought from whence the soul came, as it is upon whence the soul goeth" (3003-1). In other words, even though destiny sounds like it concerns tomorrow alone, it is actually a future that lives in the context of the past. Of special significance, according to Cayce, is the far distant past when we were created by God. The initial purpose and meaning of life at creation still provide the pattern for finding meaning in the modern world.

Cayce's ideas and theories about the creation of the human soul are complex and difficult to interpret. But for those who have an interest in this aspect of his work, appendix I has a detailed analysis of this material.

And so, with these three ingredients of broader context in mind, let's move on to the next stage of our journey to find a personal calling. Here in chapter 1 we've examined the nature of meaning, and considered how the soul's search for meaning needs to start with cooperation—cooperation that is internal (self-acceptance and self-appreciation) and cooperation with forces of destiny bigger than anyone's individual life. In chapter 2 we pick up the theme of "know thyself," which is the second lesson in Cayce's *A Search for God* soul-growth sequence.

CHAPTER 2

Self-awareness and Your Soul Talents

Father, as we seek to see and know Thy face, may we each, as individuals and as a group, come to know ourselves, even as we are known, that we—as lights in Thee—may give the better concept of Thy Spirit in this world. (262-5)

ONCE WE HAVE learned to cooperate with ourselves and the Creative Forces (as Cayce calls the divine impulse of life) and in so doing learned to truly love and appreciate ourselves, then we move on to the second step. The next challenge is to know and understand ourselves. This aspiration is beautifully expressed in Cayce's prayerful affirmation, which is keyed to the second step in the *A Search for God* sequence. It articulates the way in which we are known by higher consciousness, and it expresses the aspiration to that same kind of self-knowledge. And this lovely prayer affirms that the purpose of self-knowledge is to help us become better instruments of divine consciousness in this world.

But remember: We didn't start with self-knowledge. It's coming second here in our process of discovering a personal mission in life. Without the cooperative spirit and the self-appreciation of step one, this second step could easily turn into self-judgment and discouragement as we see things about ourselves we're not too proud of! That's why the sequencing of this unfoldment and discovery process is so important.

And so, in the philosophy of soul development in the Cayce readings, phase two is a sincere and persistent commitment to getting to know the many aspects of who we are as individuals. But self-knowledge is elusive. And just when you believe you finally know who you are, something surprises you. A strong emotional reaction seems to come from nowhere. A forgotten part of yourself pops up in a dream. Or you find yourself thinking exactly the opposite of the way you used to think about some subject.

No wonder you are an enigma to yourself. The sheer complexity of the human soul makes genuine self-knowledge a real accomplishment. You are a jumble of attitudes, feelings, beliefs, and behaviors. Often, as the well-known saying goes, "You can't see the forest for the trees." Caught up in all the competing demands of life, it's hard to get the big picture of who you really are. One moment you feel like you are a certain person with clearly defined values, plans, and ways of acting in the world; an hour later you may feel like you are someone else. Don't feel embarrassed or inadequate if you get confused about your identity. That's the human condition. Unless a person is self-realized and enlightened, he's only kidding himself to pretend that he never experiences these moments of bewilderment.

However, we don't want to glorify confusion. It may be the common state for modern men and women, but it's not the ideal for which we strive. Authentic self-knowledge is possible if we will invest the time and effort required. We never fully erase the periods of confusion about our real identity, but little by little these times of perplexity become less frequent. We begin to grow sure of a genuine character and individuality that lives within us.

It is sad to observe just how many so-called spiritual seekers are actually looking for a way to glorify their own egos. Perhaps they are not aware of what they are doing, but an unwillingness to invest time and effort in soul development leads only to self-deception. This problem has been around for a long time. Cayce's readings often chastised people for trying to take shortcuts, for trying to get around the sacrifices that are necessary in order to uncover our real spiritual being.

Sincere self-examination is a key element to Cayce's approach to finding meaning and purpose in life. In fact it is seen as the central challenge facing all of us in contemporary society. As it was said in one reading: "The greater study of self . . . should be the great study for the human family" (3744-4).

The trick is to keep self-study from turning into a preoccupation with oneself. How can an individual sincerely try to discover the true self without falling into the trap of narcissism? This is a crucial question for any spiritual discipline that claims to lead its followers to self-realization. It's the ancient problem of true and false pathways for the soul. The riddle is particularly important in these times that offer so many options for personal development, each one promising dramatic outcomes.

The Cayce readings addressed this problem. The search to find one's true self is presented as a dynamic tension between two poles—an inner and an outer. On the one hand is the inner life of reflection, self-analysis, and meditation; on the other hand is the life of relationship to the outer world and service. A true pathway for the soul—that is, one that leads to honest, objective knowledge of one's real nature—follows a balanced course. The "study of self" is looking both inward and outward.

We expect that our true nature can be discovered by looking within, but why is an outward orientation of equal importance? The answer is that the spiritual life is one of connections and relationship. The Cayce readings were very specific in regard to the purpose for which God created us as souls: companionship. That impulse for companionship is not merely with the Creator; it's for relationship with each other and even the earth.

What does that mean in practical terms? How do we gain self-knowledge through connections with other people or with the natural environment? As strange as it may sound, you can sometimes recognize your own authentic self—your own Higher Self, as it is often called—living through the words or deeds of someone else. Someone says or does something and it's as if your own best Self is communicating directly to you through that person. Or you may feel the presence of your own Higher Self living in the earth itself. You probably have this experience from time to time and don't really know what it means. It may come when you are in some natural setting: walking in the forest, weeding in your garden, sitting by the ocean. You may feel a presence that seems to communicate with you through the beauty or power of nature. That presence is something you recognize to be yourself, not your ordinary self but something that seems to come from a deeper and more genuine place within you.

The same thing may happen in relation to another person. A friend will say something profound to you, something that speaks to the deepest levels where you are struggling, yet that friend won't realize what wisdom has just come out of his or her mouth. For just a moment it's as if that friend were acting as a channel, as a mouthpiece, for your Higher Self to communicate with your normal consciousness.

Your true Self also reveals itself through interpersonal relationships when you act lovingly in service. Think of a time when you reached out to help someone simply because you cared. There was no ulterior motive. You expected nothing in return from that individual. In that act of service and loving relationship, you probably discovered something about yourself. You were awakened to a side of who you are that is easily forgotten or ignored in the modern, competitive world. That moment could never be created solely by inward reflection.

The essential point to keep in mind is Cayce's central theme of self-study. The way that we come to know who we really are is a twofold pathway. Without a doubt methods such as self-analysis, dream interpretation, and meditation are invaluable. And the other side of the coin is just as crucial. Through involvement in material life, through relationship and service, we also come to know ourselves.

Personality and Individuality

If we honestly and sincerely follow such a balanced approach to self-study, we're likely to make a discovery that the Cayce readings mentioned frequently. Each person fundamentally is made up of two parts: personality and individuality.

Personality is the mask that you wear in daily life. It's the way you appear to others, and it includes your mannerisms, your likes, and your dislikes. Personality is the product of imitation. From the moment you were born and began to observe the world around you, personality began to take shape. You learned from your parents, television, and teachers, just to name a few of the most likely influences.

Over time your personality took on a particular set of qualities that are unique to you. However, one characteristic of personality is the same for everyone: the habitual, involuntary way in which it operates. Personality runs on automatic pilot; it reacts to life situations in very predictable ways. For example, think of someone you know very well, perhaps your spouse or child. You can probably imagine a specific kind of problem for which you are sure you know how that person will react. You've seen the habitual attitude, emotion, or behavior so often in that sort of circumstance that you are positive it would happen the same way again. And as long as that person is operating from the level of his or her personality, you're right—the routine response is predictable.

Personality is not inherently good or bad. Some of the strong habit patterns we have developed are nice, and others aren't so nice. What characterizes personality is the way it operates rather unconsciously. This idea is carefully described in the writings of P. D. Ouspensky, whose work was recommended in the Cayce readings. Ouspensky wrote about the automatic, mechanical personality in his autobiography, *In Search of the Miraculous* (an account of his studies under G. I. Gurdjieff). Both Gurdjieff and Ouspensky taught that humanity in its normal waking consciousness is in a kind of sleep state relative to genuine spiritual consciousness. In other words, we move through physical life sixteen hours a day erroneously believing that we are self-conscious beings. We imagine that we frequently make free-willed choices, but the truth of the matter is just the opposite. We usually operate as a personality self and merely react unconsciously to the demands of life.

Perhaps the theory of Gurdjieff and Ouspensky sounds discouraging, yet it's found in the Cayce readings too. There are references to how our spiritual qualities are usually "slumbering" when the soul is in a physical body. Watch someone carefully; better yet, watch yourself. What you're likely to see is how readily you fall into automatic routines. You'll find you think the same old thoughts, replay the accustomed emotional patterns, spout the same familiar words, and move with consistent mannerisms. Recognizing this can even be humorous, although laughter comes more quickly when it's someone else's mechanicalness and not our own that is pointed out.

A favorite technique of comedians is impersonation. Audiences howl with delight to see the personality traits of a famous person imitated. Sometimes the joke comes from exaggerating an obvious fault in that well-known individual, but maybe there is another side to our amusement. Could we be laughing at ourselves too? Maybe something in us wakes up for just a moment when we clearly see the typical human condition.

These descriptions of the personality make it sound at best worthless and at worst an unavoidable obstacle to spiritual growth. However, it's probably necessary to have a personality to function in the world, simply because we need to be able to do certain things automatically. Driving a car, washing the dishes, or tying your shoes would be laborious if you had to make every movement with full consciousness.

The personality side of our being isn't necessarily bad or wrong; it has an important role to play if it is used properly. *The key to using it properly is getting in touch with our individuality.* This forgotten part of ourselves is our spiritual core. Many labels can be used—Higher Self, Real I, Higher Ego—but the word *individuality* nicely captures its essence. To get a better feeling for this side of ourselves, let's look at five of its qualities. They're simple to remember because each one ends with the letters *-ity*: unity, continuity, sensitivity, creativity, and activity.

The individuality of the soul bestows a profound sense of uniqueness, but paradoxically it is also in touch with the oneness of all life. The individuality is conscious of the **unity** of all creation. It directly experiences its connections with God, other souls, and the natural environment.

The individuality has **continuity** and permanence. Think about how you are in many ways a different person from who you were fifteen years ago, or fifteen years before that. And yet, in the midst of all that change, something has stayed the same. Despite all the identities that have come and gone, there is a thread of continuity. It's a dynamic continuity because even the Higher Self is in the process of development and growth. In the theory of reincarnation, the personality dissolves soon after death, but the individuality lives on.

The individuality has a **sensitivity** not just to physical influences but to the nonmaterial realm as well. It has innate intuitive abilities and can perceive things from invisible, spiritual dimensions. This natural psychic gift often operates quietly, almost behind the scenes, by gently guiding us with hunches and feelings. It presents us with a special kind of wisdom: knowing something without being able to explain how we know it.

The individuality also expresses **creativity**. Whereas the personality is caught up in routine and habit, the individuality is original and inventive. It sees life with fresh eyes and creates new responses to old difficulties. It is imaginative and able to perceive novel approaches to life. Inspired individuality brings the qualities of the infinite down into individual, finite expression.

Finally, the individuality displays **activity**. The Higher Self is not passive or hidden. Every day it is involved in life, even though the personality self may ignore its presence. The individuality constantly takes the initiative to influence conscious awareness and to provide helpful support for spiritual growth. The personality self may not want to change and may resist these overtures, but it doesn't deter the active, involved Higher Self.

Do these five qualities sound familiar? Are you in touch

with the individuality side of yourself from time to time? One good way to clarify your personal awareness of the Higher Self is to think about the very best in yourself. Take a moment to remember instances that have reflected your own excellence. They are times when you were functioning at the optimum. Don't be concerned with how frequently you have been in touch with this side of yourself; just reexperience the reality of your "individuality identity." Then think about this principle: The truth about a person is that person at his or her best. Another way of saying it is that your most authentic identity is your individuality. The other sides of you exist too, but they are more temporary—like a piece of clothing you wear for a while and then remove. The best in you is what lasts. It is the essential, spiritual core that the Cayce readings called your individuality.

Individuality and Free Will

One other characteristic of the individuality should be examined in order to get the full picture. Whereas the personality operates by routine and habit, the individuality expresses its free will. One of the most important insights from the Cayce readings about individuality is the broad and rich way in which the will is described. Nine functions of free will are described: active principle, individualizer, chooser, agent of obedience, changer, opposer of mind, developer, motivator, and guide. Let's look at them briefly, one by one. As we do, keep in mind that all of them are features of your individuality self.

1. *Active principle.* What's a good way to describe the will? Is it a special state of mind or a particular kind of energy? Or is it something so fundamental it cannot be defined in terms of other basic elements? The will is best understood as one of the three basic building blocks of the human soul. It's analogous to one of the three primary colors—red, blue, and yellow—from which other colors can be created. Together spiritual energy, creative mind, and the will form the essential trio of elements making up the soul. Therefore we cannot call the will a kind of energy or a particular state of mind. Instead the Cayce readings used the phrase "active principle" to describe its nature.

2. *Individualizer.* Free will makes each soul a unique creation. Without the will we would be robots. Just as the Cayce readings referred to "mind the builder," they also mentioned "will the individualizer." Exactly how does the will produce this uniqueness? We might wonder if the will bears the imprint of some special code that makes one person different from another, like the serial number on a dollar bill. The Cayce readings offered a different answer. The key rests with how the will makes self-reflection—that is, knowing ourselves to be ourselves—possible. Conscious self-awareness is the mark of an individualized being who has free will. As one reading put it: "The will is that birthright which makes each individual entity an *individual* soul; thus with the ability to know itself to *be* itself" (2520-1).

3. *Chooser.* This feature of the will is familiar. We make decisions using free will. However, the process of choosing among various behaviors isn't the whole story. Obviously a person may use the will by deciding to stand up rather than continue to sit down. What may not be quite so evident is the way we constantly make choices with our inner world. Every waking moment of the day we make decisions about where to place our attention. There are always choices to be made among different attitudes and feelings. As the philosopher and psychologist William James put it, the fundamental faculty of the will is the capacity to direct attention. As we choose to put attention on a particular state of mind, we feed our souls a kind of "psychic food" whose quality is based on the nature of that thought or feeling.

4. *Agent of obedience.* No doubt the word *obedience* is one of the least popular today. Everywhere we look the emphasis is on freedom to "do your own thing." Obedience sounds limiting and old-fashioned. And yet, one feature of the will is its ability to follow a higher will. This characteristic is a counterbalance to the previous one that stressed self-determination and personal choice. The will empowers us to choose freely and select our own life direction, but simultaneously it offers us another possibility: a personal **willingness** to follow God's will.

We'll see later how important this paradox of the will is. To find and live your highest purpose in life requires that you make use of both sides of your will. On the one hand, you'll need to be receptive and obedient to the mission your individuality self has accepted for this lifetime. On the other hand, that mission leaves considerable room for creative choices and decisions about exactly how you will fulfill your purpose.

5. *Changer.* Anyone on the spiritual path knows that he or she must make certain changes in order to progress. It's the will that allows changes to happen. In fact, we can alter anything about ourselves if we make a commitment to use the will in a constructive way. However, when we claim this potential for change, we should combine it with patience. Some changes cannot be accomplished immediately, and this is where much misunderstanding about the will arises. Sometimes we try to force a change according to our own timing rather than see that some patterns are deep-seated and may take a while to be transformed.

6. *Opposer of mind.* This feature of the will may sound peculiar, but it's basic to human psychology. Our minds are an extraordinary resource with talents including logical analysis, imagination, and intuition. However, the mind is also the storehouse of memory and it tends to operate in the familiar grooves etched by those memory patterns.

Our mental nature has a strong inclination to repeat the familiar and slip into predictable routines. It is only when the will comes forth to resist those habits that the higher functions of the mind—such as imagination and intuition—can emerge. We can observe one example of this process when dealing with a repeated failure. If we keep losing in some endeavor, it's easy to slip into self-pity. Feeling sorry for oneself is powerful and before long it can lead to a paralyzing depression. Only if the forces of will are mobilized is there hope. The will can oppose this trend of mind; and if it is successful, then creative, imaginative aspects of mind can surface to deal in a new way with the failure.

7. *Developer.* One Cayce reading claimed that the totality of soul development rests with the will. What a bold assertion! If everything in spiritual growth depends on the right use of will, why isn't more attention paid to this characteristic of the individuality? Perhaps it's because most people don't have as broad a definition of the will as they should. Too quickly we suppose *will* means "willpower"—that negating, suppressive impulse to force and manipulate things. Obviously willpower has little to offer spiritual development, but as the old adage warns, let's not throw the baby out with the bathwater. In this case, we must be careful we don't ignore the key to soul development just because many people misuse it.

8. *Motivator.* The will gets us moving in life. It's fine to have the right intentions and attitudes, but they're useless unless we actually do something with them. One of the purposes of life we all share is to bring spiritual qualities into individual expression in the earth. That

requires application and action. Getting motivated with the will is the starting point.

9. *Guide.* The will directs the mind. The creative potential of the mind is immense; unless an enterprise is headed in the right direction it causes only difficulties. The will is the feature of individuality that keeps the mind focused in purposeful directions. As one Cayce reading put it, "Bring self to that way of applying will wherein the Builder (the Mind) may be guided aright" (2904-1).

Model for Understanding the Personality

We've just taken a close look at the features of your most authentic self, your individuality. It's the most significant factor for living your highest purpose. However, your other side, the personality, has a role to play too. It's important to remember that the distinction between personality and individuality is not equivalent to the difference between bad and good. Calling the individuality the Higher Self doesn't mean that we should label the personality the "lower self." A better contrast would be Higher Self and "familiar self." Personality is the ordinary identity we use in most life experiences.

Let's review some of the characteristics of the personality as they were outlined earlier in this chapter. Then we'll arrange all these attributes into a model diagram that illustrates how the personality operates.

Your personality is the side of yourself produced by imitation. Over the years you have taken on patterns of thinking, feeling, and acting that you have learned from a variety of sources. It begins in earliest childhood with your parents and siblings, but the process continues into adulthood. In this sense, your personality is your *acquired* aspect, in contrast to your individuality, which is more genuinely you. Some parts of your personality are constructive or nice; other parts are weaknesses and faults.

Both personality patterns—your good side, which you're proud of, and your bad side, which you'd like to hide or change—live mainly by habit. You have little conscious control over them because they surface automatically as a reaction to events around you. If you watch your personality self closely, you'll see you are often like a finely tuned machine: Push certain buttons and you get a predictable response. Sometimes this mechanical trait is useful—for example, when you have to do some complex behavior, such as driving a car, without having to think about all the details. However, more often your mechanicalness is a serious impediment. It keeps you stuck in the same old hassles; it turns your life into an unfulfilling routine.

In order to see clearly how your personality self operates, you must notice how it is really made up of many little personalities. They might be called sub-personalities or separate "I's." Each "I" is an aspect of your personality that has its own way of thinking, feeling, and acting.

Sub-personalities are like roles you play in life—parent, employee, spouse, and so forth. The number of your different identities is even greater because each role has many versions. For example, if you are a parent you probably have several different I's that might be labeled with names like "the proud parent," "the frustrated parent," and "the demanding parent." Each one of these identities has its own strong habit patterns.

At any given moment, one of your I's has your attention. You identify with it; it's "onstage," so to speak. In that moment, all the other I's are forgotten, and the one onstage claims to answer for the whole self. However, the appearance of that sub-personality may not last long. Life conditions change and automatically a new identity grabs your attention. All day long different I's come onstage, a steady supply of shifting ways to experience yourself. One problem this condition creates is inconsistency. *It's hard to follow through on any small resolution or commitment—let alone a soul's mission—when no reliable thread of self-definition runs through your life.*

Gurdjieff used the following parable to illustrate the typical human condition, one that makes it hard to find and live your true purpose: Imagine a large house with many servants. The master of the house has temporarily departed. From time to time the telephone rings in this house and whichever servant is nearby answers. One time it may be the maid, another time the butler, the cook, or the gardener. Whoever answers the phone pretends to be the master of the house. That servant claims to be able to speak authoritatively for the entire household. However, each servant has different opinions. Someone who repeatedly calls on the telephone will no doubt be confused because each time the one claiming to be in charge has a new point of view. In the same fashion, the various I's within us try to assert authority, each one imagining itself to be more important than it is.

Perhaps the best metaphor for the personality and its many I's is a wheel. Visualize a wheel with its three principle features: rim, spokes, and hub. What would it feel like to be on the rim of a wheel as it turns? You would have the sense of movement, a perception of proceeding in a particular direction.

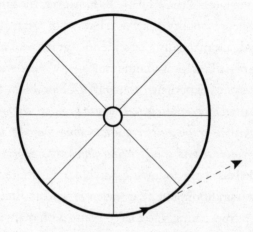

However, what feels like linear movement toward a goal turns out to be an illusion. From your point on the rim of the wheel, you would always come full circle back to the very point from which you began. In other words, the nature of a wheel is to bring things back time and again to the identical position. In exactly the same way, *your personality self continually recycles the themes of your life*. It unceasingly re-creates the same familiar issues with which you have to struggle.

For example, suppose that a man is having a hard time at his job. He feels unappreciated, he is always bickering with his fellow workers, and he's unproductive. He grows restless with this job and starts looking for another one. Assume that he puts all the blame for his problems on other people. He sees no need to change anything about himself.

Soon he finds another job and is delighted because he feels like he's really taking a step forward in his life. Has anything actually changed? The state of his inner being—his level of consciousness—attracts his circumstances. So he finds himself at a new place of employment with a new boss and coworkers. However, within a few months he will be right back in the same situation, experiencing the same problems he had before. Different people will be involved, but identical issues will arise. His personality wheel will rotate and bring him back to a familiar spot simply because he has made no changes in himself.

Think about your own past. Do you recognize any times when this has happened to you? Can you see recurrent themes created by your personality? Perhaps you'll notice that these repeating patterns usually don't make you very happy; they are detours from your true calling in life.

However, you can do something to change this situation. It begins with understanding the makeup of your personality wheel. Think of your various sub-personalities, your many I's, arranged at positions around the rim of the wheel. Each sub-personality is associated with a spoke of the wheel, and that spoke symbolizes the strong, habitual traits of that particular "I": its automatic ways of thinking, feeling, and acting.

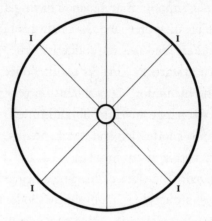

The way to free yourself from the control of this personality wheel is with a specific technique. In the Cayce readings it is called "learn to stand aside and watch yourself go by." The method is the same as the one described by Gurdjieff as self-observation. According to both of these systems of thought, the exercise is indispensable for those who want to truly know themselves and fulfill their destinies in life.

How does this technique work? Basically it is a way of waking up in life. Remember the notion that we are usually "asleep" in our daily affairs. Our eyes are open, but we are actually reacting like machines to the events around us. The wheel of personality is slowly turning and keeping us caught in habits.

Self-observation—standing aside and watching the self go by—introduces a new kind of consciousness. It involves the development of an extraordinary type of attention that focuses on two things simultaneously. With one aspect of attention we continue to be involved in events and situations around us; with another part of our attention we are acutely conscious of what we are thinking, feeling, doing, or saying. A side of ourselves stands apart from the personality wheel and looks back to witness it. Through self-observation we can wake up and begin to see clearly our various sub-personalities.

Maybe self-reflection is already something you try to do. However, for most people it's done after the fact. Hours or even days later, we may look back at something we did and observe the thoughts and feelings that led up to some behavior. That kind of self-analysis is valuable and leads to important insights, but it's not as potent as self-observation that occurs while a sub-personality is asserting itself.

Let's examine a simple example of how self-observation can work. Suppose a woman makes a firm decision to get her life on track with her authentic spiritual purpose. She's not yet clear exactly what that purpose is, but she knows where to begin: with greater knowledge of the personality side of herself. She makes a commitment to try standing aside to watch herself go by. It's not an easy discipline. The first day she remembers to do it only once, and that period of objectivity lasts for only ten seconds. The next day she totally forgets to use this technique, but on following days she becomes more consistent.

Driving home from the office, she suddenly remembers to practice self-observation. A part of her mind and attention immediately separates from the automatic self and looks back at it. The observing "I" sees that her posture driving the car is a familiar slump, a position her body habitually takes whenever she is feeling discouraged or fatigued. The observing "I" also notices an inner dialogue going on in her mind. Two sub-personalities are arguing, each one vigorously defending its own point of view. Even though the dispute is clearly a waste of time and energy, observing "I" doesn't intervene. That's not its task during self-observation. Neither does observing "I" suppress, criticize, or judge one sub-personality or another.

She is able to sustain this unusual sort of attention for a minute or two. It ends when one of her I's comes forth and is so convincing that her sense of identity is suddenly and totally captured by it. Even though she maintained this discipline for only a brief time, important spiritual work was accomplished. Another small but crucial step in self-knowledge was taken.

Over time what does she see about her personality self? She first notices how many different characters she is. Many I's live on the rim of her personality wheel. Some of the sub-personalities contradict others in their attitudes or actions. Some of her I's are rather nice or well intentioned. Other sub-personalities are more negative or disruptive. But the quality they all share is their place on the wheel of personality—their automatic, mechanical nature.

Self-observation gives tremendous self-insight, but it offers something even more valuable. Not only do we begin to see clearly the habits and routines that keep us from creative, joyful lives, but our self-observation also can start to free us from the control of the personality wheel.

How does that inner freedom arise? The key is disidentification. You rarely can change anything about yourself by fighting your faults at their own level. That sort of struggle only adds energy to the sub-personality that is giving you trouble. Change happens when you withdraw your feeling of identity from a habit—when you disidentify from it. That's exactly what happens with self-observation if it's practiced properly. Look at what happens when your observing "I" can stand aside and watch another "I" go by and do it in a loving, objective, non-judgmental way. Your observing "I" creates a remarkable feeling that says, "I have an identity *apart from* that troublesome habit." In other words, the fact that you can step aside from some part of yourself enough to witness it while it is expressing itself must mean the habit is not truly who you are.

How does self-observation help you free yourself from negative habit patterns? Don't expect success by cutting them off or trying to defeat them with willpower. Self-observation makes a more effective strategy possible. By using this method to remember your true self, you stop feeding negative habit patterns. You cut off the source that sustains them: your attention and identification with them. They slowly wither on the vine.

Let's look more closely at the goal of self-observation: to remember your authentic, spiritual self. Certainly the technique provides useful insights about the personality wheel, but even more significant is the way it can awaken the remembrance of your individuality, your Higher Self. This doesn't come immediately. It may take months of practice before one of these special moments occurs. However, with patient application you will have experiences of remembering a deeper reality about yourself. Your identity as a free, creative, spiritual being with purpose and a mission will emerge.

Those moments will inspire the same feeling you get whenever you remember something. Think about a time when you forgot someone's name and tried hard to remember it. You searched and searched your memory and then suddenly, there it was. A particular feeling came with that flash of recollection, of getting back in touch with something that you knew. That same feeling is likely to occur in self-observation when suddenly you get back in touch with who you really are: an individuality whose awareness is not caught up on the personality wheel.

For this powerful technique described by Cayce and Gurdjieff to work, it must be done properly. It promises great rewards, such as reconnection with the part of yourself that can direct the fulfillment of your purpose in life. And yet, the method is easily misunderstood or misused. One error is to assume that your observing "I" is the same thing as your Higher Self. That's not the case. Instead, the observing "I" can *lead to* the remembrance of your individuality.

Another potential error comes from making accurate self-observations but then feeling judgmental, ashamed, or guilty of what you see in one of your I's. Certainly it's true that parts of your personality wheel are negative and need to be transformed. However, judgment, shame, and guilt aren't the way to do it. That is merely a way of reidentifying with a sub-personality, and it doesn't lead to an awakening of the Higher Self. Self-observation should be practiced only with a loving, patient, and objective point of view. That's the attitude that leads to the rewards it offers.

You may feel like you're ready to give self-observation a try. Start with some little steps. Try to stand aside and watch yourself go by just once or twice a day for a minute or two at a time. Some days you may forget, but don't become discouraged. It's difficult to break the spiritual "sleep" that everyone is caught up in. On the days when you do practice the exercise, make some notes about what you observe. At first you shouldn't expect moments of remembering and directly experiencing your Higher Self. Initially the results will be useful insights about the nature of your personality wheel. You'll recognize more and more of your different I's and you'll see the habits of thought, feeling, and action that often block you from moving on to your higher purpose. Be sure to keep in mind the proper way to use this method. Observe yourself lovingly and objectively, because criticism and guilt can undermine the goal of this approach.

After considerable practice you may also discover something else about your personality wheel: the characteristic that lies in the center of the wheel. For each person this hub of the wheel is somewhat different. Gurdjieff called it the "chief feature" of the personality. In the ancient Greek tragedies, it was depicted as the fatal flaw of the hero or heroine. Whatever it may be called, it's the central misunderstanding of a person's life that lies at the heart of the personality wheel. It is a mistaken notion of life around which the various I's of the wheel revolve.

As significant as your hub of the wheel may be, it's still not very easy to see. A wise spiritual teacher who knows you well might be able to see it and describe it to you. After many years together, one spiritual mentor revealed the nature of a student's chief feature: an attitude of extreme individualism.

Perhaps what the teacher meant was that a fierce insistence to always be his own man had become a central flaw for this person—the ingredient that more than anything else could divert him from his destiny.

But what if you don't have a wise spiritual teacher? With time and persistent self-observation, you may discover for yourself the characteristic that exists in your personality as the hub of the wheel. Remember the spokes of a wheel always converge at the center. As you become more and more skillful in recognizing sub-personalities and their habit patterns, you are collecting clues that may help you to eventually see your own chief feature. It's something that you keep hidden from yourself, so it may not be easy to see. Probably it's a point in your psyche that will feel tender, even painful, when the light of conscious understanding first touches it.

Here are descriptive phrases written by several people whose serious use of self-observation finally led to break-through insights about the hub of their personality wheels. Each description defines an attitude or belief that controls the personal array of I's:

- life is made up only of one disappointment after another
- anticipation—I always have to be one step ahead of life
- control—I must always be in charge of what's going on

The fatal flaw is essentially whatever is most directly false in your personality. Most of the I's of your personality are neither good nor bad and have the potential to be useful if they are directed by the Higher Self. However, at the core of your personality wheel is something fundamentally false, something that can never lead to your real purpose in life.

It's natural to wonder, "How can I get rid of my chief feature?" Self-observation, practiced over a lengthy period, can reveal this personality flaw to you. But can you eradicate it? The best response to this discovery is to awaken your more authentic identity, your individuality. As you become clearer and clearer about who you really are, the chief feature will gradually lose influence. Maybe we can never fully destroy this false aspect of personality. Perhaps it continues to be a potential that can lead you astray, but you can free yourself of its control.

Three Seekers Deepening Self-knowledge

Let's look at the lives of three people who have successfully used ideas from the Cayce readings to find their purposes in life. We'll follow these individuals in this and the following chapters. They will serve as case studies of how to apply Cayce's strategy for finding your mission in life. Now we'll simply meet the three people and see what they discovered about themselves through self-observation.

Kate was twenty-four when she began to work with these ideas. After graduation from high school she attended a professional school of cosmetology for two years and then got a job as a hairstylist and beautician. Unmarried and having no serious romantic relationship, she hoped eventually she would have a family. When she started looking for her mission in life, she was generally happy with the way her life was going. However, she wondered if she was in the right profession, and she hoped to gain a clear vision of her purpose.

Practicing self-observation for several months, she recognized many different sub-personalities. One she labeled "the savior." It was a part of herself that felt a compulsive drive to straighten out other people's lives. Whenever she made a new friend who had some problem, she automatically assumed the role of knowledgeable helper. Even if the person didn't particularly want the assistance, this sub-personality of Kate's took the self-appointed role of counselor, worrier, and problem solver.

Another "I" she observed was "the talker." This side of herself often leapt into stream-of-consciousness talking. This sub-personality was well known to her family members and work colleagues. In fact it was a prominent part of her reputation among people. However, until she used the technique of self-observation, she had never seen just how automatically she could slip into this pattern. The most valuable insight about the talker that came through self-observation was the inner process that triggered it. To her amazement she observed that moments before the talker sprang forth, there was always a feeling of discomfort or embarrassment. The talker was an avoidance mechanism. There was nothing bad or wrong about her natural talent for conversation, except that it was being used to cover up something that needed to be confronted and dealt with: her own insecurity and need for a greater sense of self-worth.

A third prominent sub-personality she labeled "the unad-venturesome homebody." This side of herself preferred to stay in familiar surroundings. Whenever the opportunity to do something new was offered, this "I" would automatically jump out. It always had logical excuses why it was best to stay with what was customary.

Kate sensed these three I's weren't wrong—they were just parts of herself that were often misused and kept her stuck in patterns that might block her highest purpose and mission. She was able to observe those sub-personalities without be-coming overly critical of them or feeling guilty about their behavior.

Our second person is Rudy, who was fifty-nine when he began the systematic use of ideas from the Cayce readings to clarify his mission in life. He had already spent many years studying and applying several approaches to spiritual growth. A conscious search to define his life's mission may have seemed unnecessary to many of his friends. He already had a very successful career as a physician, he had been married to the same woman for more than thirty years, and they had three healthy, bright, creative adult children. Those are ex-traordinary achievements for any person in today's world. Yet something in him felt a need to see more clearly the essential meaning of his life.

Like Kate, Rudy began with the work of self-observation. He consistently remembered to stand aside and watch him-self go by in several different daily life settings. One of his significant sub-personalities was "the slave to deadlines." This side of him was driven to finish tasks on time: reports, meetings, and appointments with patients. It had its good side because it made him very reliable and competent, but it also created obstacles. Running his life like a Swiss railway schedule often blocked spontaneity—his own and that of his friends. Relationships were sometimes damaged by his sense that whatever had a deadline had top priority. He could see that certain talents and strengths that lived in that "I" had become servants to the fear of chaos and disorder.

Another "I" Rudy labeled "the compulsive nurturer." This sub-personality felt compelled to help people. Its root lay in an attitude of wanting to give rather than take from people. However, this admirable impulse had grown into certain habits that sometimes weren't very productive for Rudy or the people he tried to nurture. He observed himself repeatedly taking patients, friends, and even organizations by the hand, like a father, and leading them like children. He would make himself available day or night to those he adopted in this way. He also observed if they rejected his support, he felt terribly hurt.

A third prominent "I" was "the wise man." As a highly educated and experienced man, he could easily slip into such a role. On occasion this sub-personality was a vehicle for some of his best talents. Nevertheless, Rudy was able to see how unhealthy habit patterns had also developed within this part of himself. It was quick to get on a soapbox and expound upon the truth. This "I" also tended to ignore other wise men, or even fear that his own wisdom wouldn't be recognized and respected. His wise man wanted to be admired as a knowledgeable expert.

Our third person is Carol. A talented, multifaceted woman,

she had a varied background: writing, stage directing, psychology, and university teaching. Living now in rural Oklahoma and commuting to jobs in a big city nearby, she thought of herself as "the creative, spontaneous country woman." She was in her midthirties when she finally clarified a wording for her purpose in life, but that discovery was preceded by several years of searching.

She described herself as someone who had made it a habit to practice self-observation. What did she see? Among her sub-personalities was "the storyteller." This "I" tended to exaggerate and embellish the truth. It never actually invented a story from scratch, but simply stretched things a bit. For example, the storyteller was observed to say, "I listened to over three thousand speeches when I was teaching public speaking," when the truth was closer to two thousand. This "I" said, "He said he almost committed suicide," when in truth this friend really said he was very depressed. On the negative side this sub-personality could be seen as skillful at stretching blame and guilt, even creating major accusations out of minor infractions. But on the positive side, it was playful and often a good entertainer.

Another "I" Carol labeled "the poor baby." This sub-personality was almost totally caught up in itself. It always had words to elicit pity. It was observed to recite a litany of troubles for everyone it met: "I have so much to do; I have suffered so much." Sometimes this "I" was in charge for days at a time, but it would fade if someone would merely listen and say, "Poor baby, what a hard time you're having."

A third sub-personality Carol identified with the words

"my mother's voice." This "I" was mean to and critical of people she said she loved. It had a strong sense of how things should be done and could use humiliation or guilt to punish a different attitude or belief. This sub-personality was often seen to be a source of hurt to someone, and Carol was trying to understand it better so that she could free herself from it.

We can see from this small sampling of sub-personalities from three people—Kate, Rudy, and Carol—that we all have many roles that we switch into in the course of a day. Some of our I's are pleasant and useful; others are more troublesome. However, all the sub-personalities suffer from a common characteristic: They operate automatically. Self-observation is the first step in the process of freeing ourselves from habits that block or limit our talents and strengths.

Dealing with Negative Karma

As mentioned earlier, believing in reincarnation is an optional point of view for working with the ideas in this book. You can follow Cayce's strategy for finding your purpose in life whether or not you believe in rebirth. However, since the theory is a part of the Cayce readings, it's useful to consider one more point about reincarnation in relation to self-knowledge and your mission in life.

Some people who accept reincarnation believe the purpose of life is to atone for past misdeeds. They think they are here to clean up negative karma. They suppose their missions in life involve straightening out bad relationships, suffering through physical ailments, and putting up with assorted misfortunes—all because of misdeeds from past lives.

What did the Cayce readings say about this? On the one hand we are each responsible for what we have created in the past. Part of life, seen from the reincarnationist point of view, is to deal constructively with the karmic patterns that create our problems. On the other hand, that is not the essential mission for which each soul is born. Every one of us comes into this lifetime with a purpose that goes far beyond merely working on our own karma. We are here to serve and create.

Nevertheless, the two—negative karma to be transformed and positive missions to be fulfilled—are linked. Unless we recognize the patterns that control and limit us, they will block us from claiming the positive work of service and creativity for which we were born. This principle can be depicted in a diagram.

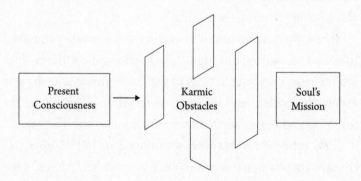

In our present state of consciousness we are seekers who want to find and live our deepest purposes. Certain patterns of attitude, emotion, behavior, and ill health can get in the way. Cayce called them karma, but we could just as easily admit that these stumbling blocks exist without resorting to a theory of past lives. These obstacles must be dealt with so we can be free to see and live the missions we came to do, but we shouldn't assume our purposes in life stop at the point of trying to purify or perfect ourselves. The relationship between self-healing and one's mission in life can be illustrated with a story taken from the Cayce files.

A thirty-eight-year-old teacher and homemaker was searching for greater understanding about her purpose in life and received a reading from Cayce. Several key talents were described, some of them with stories of past lives in which those talents were developed. In a lifetime before Christ, she had a male incarnation in which she lived on Mount Carmel as a priest, one who even came to be regarded as a sage. Long periods of meditation were a regular part of this lifetime, and the carryover effect into the twentieth-century incarnation was a strong imaginative ability.

In another incarnation—this time as a woman—she lived in a pioneer settlement along the Monongahela River. Her job was teaching the children of the community, and she was especially skilled in language instruction. This talent for teaching and words carried over into her current lifetime.

Two other aptitudes were mentioned in her reading, although they weren't accompanied by past-life stories. One was communication skills, particularly speaking; the other was the ability to encourage or discourage people.

The reading defined this woman's central life mission: to share with others through writing about her imaginative inner experiences. The reading promised she would help many individuals in this manner. However, it went on to describe a karmic pattern in her soul that could potentially undermine that mission. From yet another incarnation, certain tendencies often arose that blocked her ability to express what she was gifted to do.

Living hundreds of years ago as a man in Northumberland, England, this soul rose to leadership in a time of war and turmoil. However, in that lifetime, doubt and "the desire to be assured by others oft prevented the entity from real activity" (2520-1). We get the image of someone who was frequently paralyzed by uncertainty and overly concerned with the opinions of others. The thread of this psychological pattern was also woven into her current lifetime. Cayce characterized her this way: "At times too easily does the entity listen at what people will say, rather than to the promptings within and to that it innately knows" (2520-1).

This is an excellent illustration of the difference between a karmic pattern to be overcome and the soul purpose. Certainly this woman needed to work on her doubts and overdependence on other people. But that alone was not her mission in life. Failure to deal with this character fault could have blocked her from fulfilling the mission. She needed to always keep her eye on the deepest purpose for which she was born: to share with others through writing her imaginative inner experiences.

Inner self-study is an ongoing process. In the chapters that follow you'll start looking more directly for your mission in life. However, the job of staying in touch with your real self—the task of distinguishing between personality and individuality influences—continues throughout your lifetime. Discovering and living your soul's purpose proceeds along two parallel tracks. One is the persistent need to stand aside and watch yourself go by—self-observation that helps you get free of limiting habit patterns by remembering your real identity. The complementary path is one that you'll start in chapter 4: having faith to hear and follow your personal calling in life.

Know Thyself: What Are Your Talents and Strengths?

Everything you require to live your highest purpose in life is available to you. All you need to do is identify your inner resources and discover how to get them working together for a common aim. It takes some self-study and a lot of self-affirmation.

What about self-affirmation? Is it all right to build your self-esteem when you're on the spiritual path, or is humility the better way? Maybe the answer is that these two qualities—self-affirmation and humility—aren't mutually exclusive. The Cayce readings frequently encourage people to be more humble, but just as often, they instruct spiritual seekers to honor themselves.

A distinction, though, must be made between honoring yourself and glorifying yourself. One way to understand self-glorification is to see it in terms of the personality, as described earlier. If you glorify yourself, you identify with your personality and see yourself as better than others. And, in fact, there may well be parts of yourself that are especially skilled and capable—perhaps even far beyond the abilities of most everyone else.

However, what part of you is glorified? It's always an aspect of personality. It's not the deeper, more authentic side we have labeled "individuality." At the level of individuality we are all *equally* special. Of course, even though we share a fundamental spiritual core, differences exist from one soul to another. For example, some souls have greater spiritual maturity than others, but that doesn't make them better. In the same way, we could hardly say a teenager is somehow better than a preschooler or a full-grown tree is superior to a sapling.

Something remarkable happens whenever you remember your true identity as individuality. Suddenly there is no compulsion to compare yourself to others. There is no need to feel better about yourself at the expense of someone else. In fact, to know your true nature, to identify with your Higher Self, is to honor yourself in the sense intended by the Cayce readings. It means to recognize, respect, and commit yourself to the values and worldview of your individuality self. It means to believe your life counts—as every life does—and to accept the reality of a higher power or God.

In essence, this way of honoring yourself is harmonious with humility. Both qualities recognize the individual self is important, but *only in relationship to something bigger*. This fact is a starting point for finding the exact nature of your purpose in life. Living within you amid all the diverse, contradictory features of your personality is what one modern mystic has called an "imprisoned splendor." This Higher Self is something of tremendous beauty and power, but left to itself it has no purpose or meaning. Purpose and meaning are in relationship to other souls and to your Creator. That's the heart of humility; it's also the basis of honoring yourself.

Categories of Talents and Strengths

Each soul is born with an array of skills, strengths, and aptitudes. You, like everyone, have special talents that equip you for a creative, fulfilling life. You came into this lifetime with the assets you would need to be a success. Some of your talents have emerged naturally—abilities that simply are second nature for you. However, many other strong points have required some work or training in order to develop and mature. They have been like seeds that you were given at birth, but they sprout and grow only if you carefully nurture them.

Sometimes it may be hard for you to accept the fact that you are truly a talented person. Modern society gives extraordinary attention and publicity to just a few artists, athletes, entertainers, scholars, and politicians who excel. Sometimes it may be easy to catch yourself making comparisons and saying to yourself, "Do I really have any strong points? Isn't someone always better than I am?"

In moments like these you need another way of evaluating yourself. The issue is not whether you are the very best at some task. It's a question of what abilities you can draw upon to create and serve in the world in your own unique way. The Cayce readings redefined what it actually means to be the best at some talent. For your specific mission in life, with the people whose lives you were born to touch, you are the very best with your talents and skills. No one can live your spiritual purpose as well as you can.

One of the most fascinating parts of a Cayce life reading is its description of an individual's talents. Even the most common person is portrayed as gifted. For example, a seventy-year-old housewife was told in her reading that she had a strong will, was a good conversationalist, had a love of beauty, and was a good judge of people. A forty-year-old engineer received this portrait of his talents: skill with mechanical things, the perception of details, intelligence, and a mystical bent. A two-year-old boy was told in his life reading that he brought with him into this lifetime five assets: an aptitude for political and economic affairs, little fear of anything, communication skills, an ability to influence people, and a natural understanding of legal matters.

What is a talent or aptitude? It's a special ability that makes something come easily or naturally. It's a way that the soul and spiritual forces touch material life, a window through which creative energy and spiritual sensitivity flow into physical experience. Imagine that your Higher Self is not yet able to express itself fully in your conscious, physical life. However, a few of its qualities shine through. Your talents and aptitudes are similar to windows that let the light radiate in.

Talents are the assets you exercise in your profession. Every job requires a certain aptitude and set of skills. If your occupation demands talents that you don't have, the job is probably a strain on you. If you have abilities that aren't demanded by your profession, you may feel bored or thwarted.

Talents are just as much an issue outside a formal occupation. You draw upon your special abilities every hour of the day. These strengths and skills of your soul want to be used. In fact, you'll feel frustrated unless you make them a part of your interactions with other people.

But talents and aptitudes can be misunderstood. Some people mistakenly assume they aren't very talented because they score low on tests of intelligence. Psychologists use tests that indicate certain kinds of talent—for example, mathematical knowledge, verbal skills, or an aptitude for spatial relations—but many talents go unmeasured this way. Typical, standardized exams for intelligence are not an accurate description of your talents and aptitudes. In fact, two people with a genius-level IQ of 160 might very well have entirely different talents, just as surely as two people with IQ scores of 80.

Another mistaken notion of talents is to equate them with interests. The two can be related, but they aren't the same. Sometimes you may be interested in things that directly make use of your talents, but just as often the two may not match. Without a doubt, interests are important. They show where you're inclined to put your attention and energy. They may even indicate talents that you'd like to develop in the future.

How aware are you of the exact talents that equip you to fulfill your mission in life? Are they hidden assets buried within your soul and long forgotten? Or are they the same strong points you already know about yourself? Probably the answer is they are a mixture of both. For most people, key talents and strengths fall into these four categories: unused ones of which you are unconscious, active ones that are distorted into faults, unused ones that you know you have, and active ones that you use regularly. Let's look more closely at each category.

1. Discovering hidden talents. Have you ever thought of your soul mind as a locked treasure chest? In many ways it is, because you have within yourself forgotten and unclaimed knowledge and abilities. A few of those talents may be important ingredients that you'll use for living your spiritual purpose. How do you get in touch with these treasures?

One method is to remove the barriers that have gotten in the way. Perhaps an experience earlier in life convinced you that you were awkward or untalented in some area. Often this happens in childhood. That unpleasant experience may still live—either as a conscious memory or as an unconscious block—and keep you from claiming the real ability that is yours. But removing these barriers is easier said than done. It may require you to forgive someone—yourself or a person who criticized you. Or it may necessitate that you encourage other people who are trying to overcome a similar obstacle. It's an amazing fact of personal development that helping someone else often stimulates healing within yourself.

Another method for connecting with forgotten talents is to listen to your unconscious. In meditation or dreams you may catch a glimpse of a hidden ability. As you quiet your personality self in the silence of meditation and become receptive to your individuality, you may get in touch with a particular strength of your soul. This is exactly what happened to some people who joined a prayer study group founded by Edgar Cayce. In meditation a few members of the group obtained intuitive impressions of certain healing talents. Later during readings given by Cayce, they asked about the validity of what they had received. They were told that these were authentic abilities ready to be claimed and developed.

In a dream you may find yourself skillfully doing something that has never been part of your self-image. For example, a man who received many Cayce readings worked as a New York City stockbroker. He had all the necessary skills for that and was very successful. Then he started to notice his dreams. Frequently they portrayed him using a different kind of ability than he used in his job. Recurrently he dreamed that he was lecturing before large audiences on the subject of spiritual truth. In most of the experiences he was eloquent and impassioned; however, in some of the dreams he was presented with the opportunity to share his philosophy but was unsure of himself, remembering his lack of academic credentials. Readings were given to decipher these dreams. Cayce's interpretation was that the man's mission in life involved the creative use of this talent for verbal expression of spiritual truth. The readings urged him to claim this ability and not limit himself merely because of missing college degrees.

A third method for discovering your hidden talents is to be adventuresome. Try activities for which you don't think you have a natural talent. You may surprise yourself. You may not paint like Rembrandt or Picasso the first time you pick up a brush, and you may not write poetry like Whitman the first time you scribble down a verse, but an adventuresome spirit could produce great rewards. Even though some experiments will only confirm suspicions that you lack certain talents, one or two surprises may await you. When you uncover a promising ability, next comes a willingness to invest time in training and practice so that the natural talent can emerge. Aptitudes and strengths of the soul sometimes blossom on their own with little or no effort on our part. On the other hand, a talent that has remained unconscious well into adulthood is likely to need some work to coax it forth and polish it up.

2. Reclaiming strengths hidden in faults. Paradoxically, a second category of talents involves a careful look at faults and weaknesses. This probably seems like an unlikely place to find abilities and aptitudes, but it's right where the Cayce readings suggest you might find some.

This concept is based on Cayce's somewhat radical view of good and evil. Obviously this is a profound issue that extends far beyond questions of how you can identify your talents. Theologians and philosophers have wrestled with the problem of good and evil for centuries. Could the Cayce readings have had anything new to offer? Maybe so.

This material proposes that evil is real. Forces exist in the universe that can lead you away from your true purpose and destiny. Those forces exist both outside you and within you. But what is evil? What is the essential nature of something you call "bad" in yourself or in the world around you? According to the Cayce readings, "Bad is good gone wrong"

(1201-2). For example, what you might call a fault in yourself or someone else could be seen in a different way. It's a strength or asset that unfortunately has been distorted, overdone, or misused. The basic goodness has been hidden, but it's still there.

In what may well be the most challenging statement made in any Cayce reading, the following idea is presented: The essence of pure goodness can be found even in the most despicable behavior. Perhaps that sounds incredible to you. Your mind may race to find an exception to the rule, some action so bad that surely nothing admirable could be buried like a seed there. Why is it such a natural response to resist this idea? Shouldn't we find it hopeful? Certainly this principle says we should be more patient and tolerant of other people and their faults, but it also shows a new way of seeing our own weaknesses.

Suppose one of your faults is being judgmental. You're aware of this trait and you call it bad. You can't deny that it needs to be changed. It causes unnecessary problems for you and everyone around you. What does Cayce's challenging idea say about this fault? There is the seed of something good in your judgmental nature. A talent or strength of your soul has been distorted, overdone, or misused, and it comes out looking this way. Even though this fault needs to be corrected, it indicates there is an important asset you can reclaim. Maybe that hidden strength is discernment. Perhaps you have a talent for clearly evaluating things, but it's distorted by a tendency to measure other people by your own values and standards. In this example, the ability to discern might have an important role to play in fulfilling your purpose in life. You don't want to overlook this ability merely because you have distorted it or misused it in the past. The fault needs to be lovingly corrected but in such a way that you recapture something very valuable for yourself.

3. *Getting talents into the thick of action.* No athlete wants to be a benchwarmer. It's frustrating to have ability and not get into the game. In a similar way, you are "coach" of a "team" that is made up of your talents and abilities, and you often keep some of them on the bench. You know you have certain abilities, but you never get around to using them. Why? Lots of excuses come to mind. "I'm too busy" and "I'm not sure I'm good enough" are two frequent reasons why a talent stays out of action.

These "benchwarmer" talents are often ones that no one knows you have. They represent secrets you've kept to yourself. An analytical research scientist may know she has a gift for dance, but she never seems to find the time or the self-confidence to let that ability shine. A sophisticated businessman may suspect that he has a knack for being playful and fun-loving with children, but somehow that talent never gets a chance to prove itself.

Another excuse often relegates a strength to benchwarmer status: the fear it might take your life in a new direction. The research scientist may fear she would find dance so enjoyable she would want to abandon her current job. The businessman might worry that spending time with children would make him lose his tough, competitive edge.

It's unfortunate when you cut yourself off in this way. Any

talent with which you were born has a place in your life. Its role isn't to be disruptive and force you to change, unless the patterns of your life are out of sync with your real purpose. These benchwarmers deserve a chance to be recognized and to get into the game occasionally.

4. Liberating your familiar talents from a rut. Most of your talents and aptitudes are ones that you use at least occasionally. Significant ones are indispensable to the way you run your life. These skills, abilities, and aptitudes are so much a part of you that friends immediately think of these characteristics when your name is mentioned. It's safe to say that such talents have some important role to play in your spiritual mission.

A problem may arise, however. Familiar abilities can easily slip into routine ways of being used. Returning to the metaphor of the personality wheel, imagine how many of your most prominent strengths exist as spokes on your wheel. They have become closely linked with particular sub-personalities, and they usually function on automatic pilot. Even though they still have the potential to be great strengths, their potency is diminished as soon as they get captured in the mechanical routines of personality.

Try to observe this process in yourself. Think of one of your more positive I's and identify its strengths and talents. What do you see? Does that sub-personality possess a gift for organization, dependability, or wit? Maybe it exhibits spontaneity, empathy, or logic. Whatever features you recognize, they are probably some of your best points—characteristics you are proud to have. And yet, if those traits have become routine and predictable, they have lost much of their power. The wheel of personality can drain them of their vitality. They may lose their spiritual force for helping you fulfill your purpose in life.

To understand the significance of this problem, try the following exercise. Take a piece of paper and a pencil and record some self-observations. Begin by writing "My greatest strengths" at the top of the page. Then make a list of the most obvious talents and abilities of the I's on your personality wheel. Stop reading here until your list is complete.

Now erase the word *strengths* at the top of the paper and replace it with the word *obstacles*. Think of the items on this list as your greatest obstacles to growth.

How did you react to this shift in perspective? Have you ever thought of your strengths and talents as hindrances? This exercise may exaggerate, but it makes a compelling point. You can get so locked in to the habits of your personality self— even your positive ones—that they become a barrier. They can make you deaf to the inspirational prompts of your individuality self. Your familiar strengths can become so fixed in routine that they lose their ability to respond to a higher, spiritual direction. Instead of talents serving a mission in life, they can actually resist it.

The answer to this dilemma is to bring the wheel of personality under the direction of the Higher Self. As you become more and more conscious of your individuality self, your talents have a new source of purpose and direction. They are liberated from the wheel of routine and habit. By reclaiming the talents and aptitudes you already know you have, by bringing them under the direction of your more authentic self, you take a big step toward your mission in life.

These talents are especially important to fulfill your calling. For most people this fourth category accounts for 80 to 90 percent of the skills they need to draw upon in living their missions in life. Most of the ingredients you need to express your highest purpose probably are abilities already known to you. The trick is to regain mastery of them, to rescue them from familiar routines, habits, and ruts.

Identifying Your Talents and Strengths

Every soul shares a common purpose: to express the infinite in the finite. Now, as a playful analogy, imagine that the purpose of life—yours and everyone else's—is to bake bread. We are all here in the physical world with a mission to be bakers. However, our mutual calling to be bakers of bread doesn't end with such a generality. Each of us is here to specialize and become a master baker of one particular type of bread—whole wheat, rye, cinnamon raisin, sourdough, pumpernickel, and so forth. We each have a specialized mission within the context of the shared purpose of life.

What kind of bread are you called to bake? Before you decide, it might be a good idea to check the cupboard in your kitchen and see what ingredients you have available. If you speculate that your expertise will be in baking cinnamon raisin bread, only to discover your cupboard lacks those two key elements, then your chances of success are nil. This is a simple analogy, but it illustrates the usefulness of taking an inventory of your talents and strengths before trying to formulate a statement of your life's purpose. Your aptitudes provide invaluable clues.

You'll want to have a piece of paper and pencil for the next few steps. They involve compiling a list of your most prominent abilities. As you work on these exercises, avoid false modesty. This is not the time for selling yourself short. Humility is a virtue, but it's artificial if it denies the essence of your spiritual nature, your talents.

Try each of the four steps described below. You may get good results from all four, or you may find only one or two of the approaches feel right for you. Use your own good judgment in evaluating what you get. At the end of the fourth step, write down a composite result of these exercises. It will be a list of your talents, abilities, aptitudes, skills, and strengths. Most people end up with a list comprising eight to fifteen entries. Any fewer than that and you're probably not giving yourself enough credit. Any more and you're probably not staying focused on your most significant abilities.

1. Review previous successes. What are your most significant achievements? Think back to your childhood and adolescence as well as adulthood. In what activities have you been a success? Some of the experiences that come to mind may be noteworthy because you were recognized for what you accomplished. Maybe you won an award, earned a certificate, or received praise. Other experiences that are just as important may have gone unrecognized by other people. Only you know about those successful accomplishments.

For each achievement that you recall, analyze your formula for success. What talents, strengths, and abilities did it take to accomplish the task? For example, earning a college degree may have required persistence and writing skills; raising a child may have demanded love and tolerance; overcoming a phobia may have necessitated courage and good humor.

2. Examine three categories of talent. One system of thought—described in Richard Nelson Bolles's classic book on career guidance, *What Color Is Your Parachute?*—proposes that virtually all talents fit into one of three categories: skills with people, skills with things, and skills with information.

Skills with people starts with basic abilities such as taking instruction or serving. More advanced abilities demand greater interaction—talents such as communication, persuasion, and supervision. The highest level of skill for dealing with people includes negotiating, leading, counseling, and training.

Skills with things must be viewed broadly to include machines, nature, and the physical body. The fundamental skills in this category include handling objects, bodily strength or agility, working the earth, and monitoring or tending machines. More advanced abilities include operating machines, using tools, and repairing mechanical devices.

Skills with information starts with observing, comparing, copying, and computing. More sophisticated skills in this category include researching, analyzing, organizing, and evaluating. The most advanced type of information skills are visualizing, creating, and designing.

Although this is just a sketch of an elaborate theory, it may get you started on some new insights about your own talents. Think about each of these three categories. What are your strengths when it comes to dealing with other people? With physical objects? With information? You might find it useful to take a piece of paper and make three columns. At the top of the page put a label for each category, and then write down your skills and abilities under the appropriate headings.

3. Reclaim strengths within faults. Remember one of the four categories of talent described earlier is hidden strengths embedded in personality faults. Sometimes it's not easy to see the essential goodness buried in one of your weaknesses, but it's worth the search.

Make a brief list of about five or six of your faults. For each one try to experience a new point of view about that shortcoming. Get beyond guilt, self-condemnation, and defensiveness. Objectively look at each fault and ask yourself, "What talent or strength is here, although it's distorted, misused, or overdone?" For example, you might discover idealism buried in your impatience with others, or passion hiding in your worrisome nature, or spontaneity buried in disorganization.

Don't be concerned if you can't find a strength in every weakness. Occasionally it takes a long time before you can catch a new perspective on some fault. The buried talent may be very distorted. Even though you may reclaim just a few talents with this technique, it's a valuable method that shouldn't be ignored.

4. Survey a list of sample talents. Some possibilities may stimulate your thinking. Scan the following two collections of sample talents, strengths, aptitudes, and skills. Notice which ones jump out at you. Keep in mind these inventory lists are incomplete and contain only examples of assets you might possess. One entry may remind you of another talent that isn't on the list. The first list contains adjectives that may describe you; the second list describes specific skills.

PERSONAL DESCRIPTIVE ADJECTIVES

adventurous	*financially adept*
articulate	*flexible*
artistic	*focused*
assertive	*forgiving*
astute	*friendly*
committed	*generous*
conscientious	*honest*
consistent	*imaginative*
cooperative	*industrious*
courageous	*initiating*
creative	*innovative*
decisive	*inspiring*
dependable	*intuitive*
discerning	*kind*
disciplined	*logical*
dynamic	*loyal*
easygoing	*mechanically skilled*
empathetic	*modest*
energetic	*musical*
enthusiastic	*objective*
experimenting	*open-minded*

optimistic

orderly

organized

patient

peaceful

perceptive

persistent

persuasive

physically coordinated

playful

poised

practical

productive

psychic

risk-taking

self-reliant

sensitive

sincere

spontaneous

steady

tactful

tolerant

trustworthy

wise

witty

zealous

Personal Skills

caring for animals

caring for children

concentrating

cooking

gardening

having a sense of humor

leading

listening

motivating

negotiating

planning

synthesizing

teaching

troubleshooting

writing

Now take a blank piece of paper and make a list that summarizes your best answers to these four exercises. If one exercise was especially useful, you may find the majority of items on your final inventory come from that one approach. Remember, you are trying to create a list with at least eight but probably no more than fifteen entries.

Prioritizing Your List of Talents

Take another look at your list of abilities. It's impressive, isn't it? Don't feel as if you're bragging—admit you're a pretty talented person, whether the world around you realizes it yet or not.

The items on your list are the ingredients within your soul that have an important role to play in living your highest purpose and mission. However, some of the talents are more crucial than others to success. A few of them are particularly significant because they play such a big part in shaping the nature of your calling, your spiritual vocation.

The fact that just a few talents have a special priority doesn't diminish the value of the others. It simply means a few of your abilities are particularly influential in shaping your calling in life. This point can be illustrated with an example from sports. The 1927 New York Yankees are one of the most famous baseball teams of all time. Some people believe they were the greatest baseball team ever assembled. Two star players were Babe Ruth and Lou Gehrig, both of whom were elected later to the Hall of Fame. Those two extraordinary players shaped the character of the team with their nearly unstoppable hitting. But they couldn't have won the World Series that year by themselves. Every player on the team had a role to play. Some made a small contribution, but it was a total team effort that made the 1927 Yankees a success.

In exactly the same way, you have certain talents that are more important than others to your mission in life. They shape the basic character of what you were born to do. Other strengths and abilities have a job too, but they assume a supplementary function in helping you to live your purpose.

How many key talents do you have? A good guess is four. This is the average count of strengths and abilities described in a Cayce life reading. In some readings there are just three; in others, five or six. However, when we look at the hundreds of life readings as a whole, four is about the norm.

What does this suggest about the way your soul came into physical life? You brought with you a few critical assets for success in your mission. You can think of those talents as gifts from God or as abilities developed in previous lives. If you had been fortunate enough to receive a Cayce life reading, you would have been able to use the distinctive strengths it described as key ingredients throughout your life to fulfill certain purposes. Of course those four abilities aren't the limit of your assets. As you've already seen by compiling a list of talents and strengths, you have far more resources to draw upon than just four. Soon after birth you started learning new abilities to complement the ones with which you were born.

How can you recognize the four most significant strengths from among the others on your list of eight to fifteen talents? Several approaches may be effective for you. First, look back at your childhood. Presumably your essential character as a soul was close to the surface when you were young. As you grew older your personality developed more and more fully; the imitative side of you began to assert greater control—both the negative habits you picked up as well as the strengths you acquired through learning.

What were you like as a young child, especially in the years before you started school? If you don't remember very well, perhaps you can collect memories from your parents or older siblings. Sometimes one or more of your key talents were evident during earliest childhood. They may have appeared as a strong interest or a natural aptitude for some activity. For example, did you have an artistic flair as a youngster, or a knack for mechanical things? Did you love music or have a vivid imagination?

Second, reconsider your longer list of eight to fifteen talents. Ask yourself, "Do any of these abilities seem to be right at the core of my being? Is there one talent that's so essential that it's hard to imagine being me without it?" When one of your personal assets feels that important to you, it's likely to be one of the key strengths that is crucial to your life's mission.

Third, try another questioning approach. Often the talents that are most significant to your purpose will have a feeling of "unfinished business" until they are fully utilized. Look again at your list of talents. Do any of them seem to speak to you about unfinished business? Is there one that gives you a feeling of unrealized possibilities, saying, "I'm not through with you yet, and you're not through with me"?

All three approaches are likely to give you some clues. One of the exercises may work especially well for you, but be sure to take a little time for each. When you've had a chance to speculate about your four most important abilities, make a tentative choice. With a feeling of playful experimentation, circle four of the items on your longer list. Imagine these are the four that Edgar Cayce would have mentioned in a life reading given for you. You'll build upon these four later as you start clarifying the exact nature of your calling in life.

Let's examine the insights of the three individuals introduced earlier in this chapter. They followed the same steps, trying to recognize their own most important talents.

Kate, the twenty-four-year-old beautician, compiled a list of ten talents and strengths by completing the four exercises. Next, she narrowed it down to the four that were most likely to influence the nature of her mission in life. The four she chose were sensitivity, a sense of humor, a friendly nature, and an eye for beauty.

Sensitivity made it to her original list of ten abilities because she recognized it as a strength within a fault. She was the sort of person who easily got her feelings hurt—a constant problem to her friends, her family, and herself. However, when she looked at this shortcoming in a new way, she saw a strength that was being misapplied. She was a highly sensitive person and that sensitivity didn't have to be distorted by a lack of self-esteem. This newly recognized ability was chosen for her final list of four because it felt like it was right at the core of her being, an essential part of her individuality.

A sense of humor was an entry on the personal skills list. It stood out for her as she scanned the list. When it came time to narrow her compilation of talents from ten to four, this one had the feeling of unfinished business. It felt to Kate as if her sense of humor was a resource she was just beginning to tap.

She wrote down "a friendly nature" on her original list when she reviewed the three categories of talents. When she considered people skills, this one immediately seemed prominent. Later she selected it as one of the most important four because of childhood recollections. Her earliest memories were overtures to strangers who visited her home. As a preschooler she was invariably outgoing and quick to make friends.

An eye for beauty was already a source of accomplishments in her life. It had led her to successful training as a beautician. For example, even though she wasn't born knowing how to cut and style hair, a natural aptitude made the skills come easily. Later this ability made possible some achievements and recognition in the first years of her professional career. She chose this particular talent as one of her final four because it had a feeling of unfinished business. It seemed her eye for beauty could be used to enrich her own life and that of others in ways she hadn't discovered yet.

Rudy, the physician, narrowed his more lengthy list of talents down to leadership, teaching, planning, and courage. Leadership made it onto his original list of abilities because of previous accomplishments. He had a history of taking the initiative for causes in which he believed. In the early 1960s he led a small group of professional people concerned about the unrecognized hazards of fluoridation in drinking water. His leadership helped bring the issue to a public vote in his home city, one of the ten largest in America. Several years later he demonstrated his leadership abilities by founding a private school for children based on a curriculum that recognizes the spiritual dimension of each student. This particular talent seemed to be so much at the core of his being that it warranted a place among the final four.

Teaching also appeared on his longer list of skills because of previous successes. For nearly twenty years he taught part-time at a nearby medical school. Using that ability had always given him a great deal of pleasure, and he had received several commendations for excellence. He selected teaching as one of his most important talents because it had the feeling of unfinished business. As successful as he had already been in teaching medical students, he still had the intuition that his teaching could reach other types of people and focus on new subjects.

As Rudy reviewed the three fundamental areas in which skills find expression—with people, with things, and with information—one that stood out was his ability to organize information for planning purposes. He saw how this was a natural aptitude that came in handy in parts of his life ranging from a business plan for his medical clinic to designing a vacation trip. This skill seemed like a worthy candidate to be one of his four most important because it seemed to be so clearly at the core of his being. Virtually all of his friends and family members tended to think of this ability if they were asked to describe his character.

Just as quickly those same friends and family would have added that one of Rudy's faults was to be pushy and demanding, both of himself and of others. He readily admitted to that short-coming but was able to see that it also contained the seed of a great strength, which he was able to express in purer form on a regular basis. Since his youth Rudy had exhibited his courage. He repeatedly demonstrated a willingness to face his fears and push himself to go beyond them, sometimes picking a task for himself simply because he knew it would be difficult. In relationships he often slipped into expecting the same from those around him. Sometimes it proved to bring out the best in someone; other times, the individual backed off, feeling pushed. Yet despite the fact that in the past this talent had not always been used in the best ways, it still deserved a place on his list of four significant abilities.

Carol, the "creative, spontaneous country woman," selected these four talents as most significant: writing, sensitivity to feelings, creativity, and an ability to see the big picture. Writing had been a frequent source of accomplishment in both professional and avocational settings. She saw it both as a way of communicating clearly and as therapy for herself. At the same time she felt ways still remained for her to make optimal use of that skill. There was unfinished business between her and this aptitude for writing.

One of her abilities in dealing with people was an innate sensitivity to what is going on under the surface. She used this skill as a child to help her win prizes selling items door-to-door in the neighborhood. She could immediately sense a customer's personality and needs, which allowed her to say just the right thing to make a sale. This talent was further sharpened by graduate school training and job experience in nonverbal behavior, game theory, communications, and theater direct-ing. This talent seemed to be right at the core of her being. Often she observed this sensitivity to unspoken feelings and how it led her to say just the right thing at the right time, guided intuitively rather than by logically figuring out what ought to be said.

Since her youth Carol had had a tremendous creative im-pulse. Occasionally this strength came out as a weakness in her temperament: a tendency to get bored easily. However, on occasion both she and others recognized her creative spark for what it was: a great ability for making something new out of old situations and resources. This talent came forth in the-atrical work, college teaching, and relationships. For her it was obviously one of her most important assets.

Perhaps related to her creativity is another talent that she listed as one of her final four: the capacity to see the whole picture. Once again she was able to identify a critical skill because of previous accomplishments with it. Some of her most satisfying interactions with friends—relationships in which she felt like she had truly been able to help—were those in which she could see how the fragments of someone's life could be put together in a meaningful way. In her theater work, what made her good as a director was this capacity to keep the big picture in view all the time. This talent is indis-putably a versatile one and bound to be an asset in most any kind of career or interest. For this reason it had the feeling of unfinished business: Opportunities remained for it to be used in new ways.

Like these three people, you have formulated your own

inventory of talents and strengths. You've narrowed your longer list of eight to fifteen skills and abilities down to about
four that probably have the greatest role to play in shaping
the character of your soul's purpose. In chapter 4, several exercises will help lead you from that short list of talents to a
succinct statement of your mission in life. However, before
you leave this chapter on abilities and strengths, keep in mind
that all of your talents will have some role to play in how you
bring your mission to life. The situations and opportunities
you encounter are so varied that every asset within your soul
has a creative place to be used.

CHAPTER 3

Values, Ideals, and Intentionality

*God, be merciful to me! Help Thou my unbelief! Let me see in Him
that Thou would have me see in my fellow man. Let me see in my
brother that I see in Him whom I worship.* (262-11)

WITH A COOPERATIVE spirit that cultivates self-love and
self-appreciation, and with a deeper sense of self-knowledge
and one's own gifts and talents, we are able to choose a moral
compass for life. Having taken those first two steps in the *A
Search for God* soul-growth sequence, you are now able to do
an effective job in answering the question "What is my ideal?"

It's difficult to understand Cayce's view of life unless we
appreciate the importance he gave to ideals and purposes.
However, it's important to remember that whenever Cayce
spoke of ideals he meant something more profound than just
socially acceptable rules and shallow moralistic platitudes.
The transformational psychology and the philosophy of spiritual growth that can be found in his teachings emphasize
the dynamic importance that intentionality has upon all of
one's life experience. What one holds as an intention or an
ideal is a powerful and lively factor in shaping our thoughts

and emotions—and, in turn, our experiences in material life. By establishing a clear and heartfelt spiritual ideal, we set the stage for what will come next: experiencing the call of one's purpose in life.

It might be tempting even to say that everything *starts* with ideals, but, in fact, the lesson from the *A Search for God* material titled "What Is My Ideal?" comes third in the sequence rather than first. Initially, we need to nurture that deeply cooperative relationship with ourselves and the Creative Forces. Second, we need to really get to know ourselves—both the mundane personality self (and all its sub-personalities or I's), as well as the more authentic individuality self. Once those two steps have been accomplished, we can fruitfully make a decision about core values and a personal spiritual ideal. And as we see here in the prayerful affirmation that Cayce gave for meditation on the third step—What Is My Ideal?—his sense of *how* we form an ideal is closely related to our capacity to *see the good in life all around us, especially the best in other people.*

The Ideal and Guidance to Discover a Mission

The journey to find and live a soul purpose includes clarifying one's deepest values. The ideal serves as a compass that points the way; then, the mission statement will articulate the specifics of where one is headed along that direction.

Ultimately, this process to hear one's calling is a matter of *spiritual guidance.* The core values one sets for his or her life have a tremendous influence on the quality of guidance one receives, in addition to the powerful role that that ideal plays in evaluating and applying the guidance. This is especially true when it comes to guidance about the nature of one's calling and life purpose.

An ideal is crucial to the guidance process because within oneself there are so many contradictory opinions and points of view, each clamoring to be the primary source of direction. Just think back to the last time you had to make a difficult decision. If you carefully watched your feelings, rational analysis, and intuitions about the matter, you may have felt as if you were fighting your way through a jungle of diverse options. You probably needed something like a machete to cut through the tangle and see your way free to move ahead. A clearly articulated ideal is that tool.

Or consider another metaphor. Sometimes a problem in life leaves us feeling as if we're in a fog, adrift on a turbulent ocean. The fog symbolizes the many confusing options that come to mind in trying to deal with the problem. An ideal is like a beacon that shines brightly through the mist and indicates a path home. Through the many layers of the mind, an ideal serves like a lighthouse guiding a ship over stormy, foggy seas.

We all want our decisions and choices to be good ones; that's why we even consider the need for guidance—be it from a counselor, *The I Ching,* a dream, or any of the other avenues for getting direction. We want direction that bears good fruits—a more fulfilling and healthy life for us *and* those around us. And that is what is most likely to come if we have formulated a clear and distinct sense of a personal spiritual ideal or core values.

A Model for Understanding Ideals

The Cayce philosophy includes a fascinating concept about dimensions of consciousness. Although this has often seemed complex and abstract to many people, the elegance and simplicity of this model of human consciousness shows us exactly why ideals are critical to spiritual guidance.

Consider first the notion that our normal, waking consciousness is three-dimensional. Our perception of reality is by and large focused on the physical world, and our minds tend to understand things in terms of three measurements. For example, we see time as threefold: past, present, future. We see space as threefold too: height, width, and depth. Modern physics *and* the teachings of mystics suggest that time and space may be much more complex than our everyday conscious minds think; but for the most part, three-dimensional consciousness serves us well day in and day out.

What is the next higher dimension? On this point, Cayce and Jung agree. It's the realm of ideas or thoughts.

Best definition that ever may be given of fourth-dimension is an idea! Where will it project? Anywhere! Where does it arise from? Who knows! Where will it end? Who can tell!

It is all inclusive! It has both length, breadth, height and depth—is without beginning and is without ending! Dependent upon that which it may feed for its sustenance, or it may pass into that much as a thought or an idea. Now this isn't ideal that's said! It's idea! see? 364-10

If we wished to form a vivid picture of a non-spatial being of the fourth dimension, we should do well to take thought, as a being, for our model.*

In other words, the mental realm has reality, which in many ways is just as genuine as the physical world (or maybe more so). As Cayce put it:

For, thoughts are things! and they have their effect upon individuals, especially those that become supersensitive to outside influences! These are just as physical as sticking a pin in the hand! 386-2

At first it may take a little effort to appreciate the reality of this thought-form world. Where is a thought? What does it look like? How can it be real if you can't grasp or measure it? Consider this example: What makes this book you are reading real? Is it the weight of the paper and the color of the ink? That's a superficial way of looking at it. A more profound answer to this question says that it's the *ideas* in the book,

---

* C. G. Jung, *Modern Man in Search of a Soul* (Boston: Houghton Mifflin Harcourt, 1955), 184.

ideas that come to life in your mind as you read. What's more, the same idea can be shared with any number of other people scattered throughout the world, and even throughout generations. An idea isn't limited to space or time.

Via the fourth dimension we discover the extraordinary power of the mind. We experience the amazing creative potential of our thinking—that we can literally create miracles by our thoughts (or, as one Cayce passage warns, we can also create serious crimes with our thinking). Fourth dimensionally we find that we are connected to each other. ESP works largely by this higher dimensional bridge from person to person. What's more, *the fourth dimension is the source of the third.* Over the years we have created a physical reality out of our attitudes, thoughts, and emotions. In this sense, the Cayce philosophy says that the third dimension is a projection of the fourth— that "Mind is the builder, and the physical is the result."

But the fourth dimension also has the potential to be a morass. It contains many different perspectives and options of human consciousness; many of them are expansive and liberating, but others are self-centered and ultimately unhealthy. One can easily get lost amid the fascinating array of possibilities offered by the unconscious mind, and this becomes a critical issue whenever we try to engage inner tools for guidance, such as dreams, meditation, hypnosis, or intuitive impressions. Something more is needed if we are to find our way reliably through all the possibilities. That something more is the next dimension.

The fifth dimension is an ideal. Whereas an idea (i.e., the

fourth dimension) is the specific mental construct of an attitude, thought, or emotion, a fifth-dimensional ideal is the
motive, purpose, or value that stands behind that fourth-
dimensional idea. Remembering how the third dimension of
physical reality can be understood as a projection coming
from the next higher dimension (where "mind is the builder"),
a similar relationship exists between the fourth and fifth dimensions. An idea, thought, or emotion is a projection of some
overarching purpose, motive, value, or ideal (i.e., the stuff of the
fifth dimension).

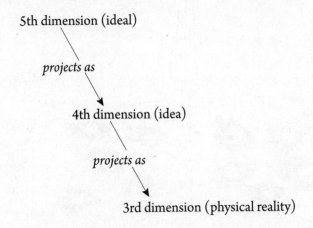

5th dimension (ideal)

projects as

4th dimension (idea)

projects as

3rd dimension (physical reality)

But what does all of this have to do with spiritual guidance
and the discovery of one's calling in life? Simply using the guidance tools that draw upon the fourth dimension isn't enough.
Studying our dreams, listening for guidance in meditation, allowing synchronicity to point the way, or any other methodology
still requires something that helps us sort through all the images,

impressions, and feelings that arise. This is where a personal spiritual ideal (the fifth dimension) plays such a helpful role.

Like a lighthouse beacon, it moves us through the variety and complexities of the fourth dimension. And as it draws us through, we can pick up along the way the fourth-dimensional images, insights, and inspirations that we need, the ones that are consistent with that fifth-dimensional ideal we've set.

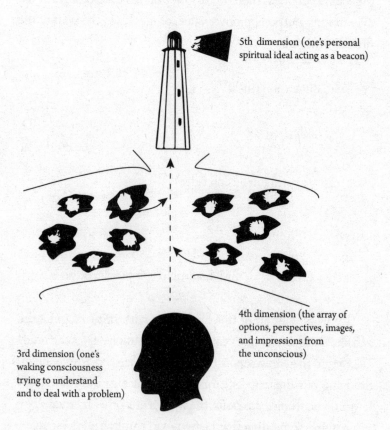

5th dimension (one's personal spiritual ideal acting as a beacon)

4th dimension (the array of options, perspectives, images, and impressions from the unconscious)

3rd dimension (one's waking consciousness trying to understand and to deal with a problem)

A Psychology of Ideals

As already suggested, anyone who has studied the Cayce teachings knows the importance of motives, purposes, and ideals. For example, the approach to meditation advocated in this material is essentially ideals-centered. What's more, Cayce's elaborate theory of dream interpretation largely rests on the assumption that the dreaming mind uses one's own ideals to *shape dream experiences*. In order to interpret many dreams we can ask what sort of ideal or motivation each symbol represents. The dream as a whole can be addressed with the question "What do I see about my life when I compare the action in my dream to what I hold as an ideal for my life?"

Cayce's pioneering work with natural healing methods and holistic health also rests on a foundation of ideals and motives for the client. The person who wants to get well needs to have a sense of purpose in life. As Cayce often asked those who came to him for guidance about healing, "What do you want to do with your life and your healthy body once the ailment has been cured?" Those who didn't have a good answer weren't very likely candidates for his healing methodologies.

The most-quoted Cayce passage about ideals comes from advice to a forty-year-old woman working as a clerk during World War II. "Then, the more important, the most important experience of this or any individual entity is to first know what *is* the ideal—spiritually" (357-13).

Cayce described an essential human dilemma. Our minds— with extraordinary creative potential—are pulled in two directions. In one direction is the attraction of an ideal, a positive, creative image of what is possible; in the other is the tug of material desires. Unfortunately it's those limiting, self-serving material influences that frequently gain the upper hand.

How do those desires that are focused on materiality gain our attention? Usually it's either by (1) crises and emergencies or (2) good excuses and rationalizations. Think about your own life in those terms. What interrupts or diverts you? What interferes with the pursuit of your ideals? For most of us, it's an endless stream of material life demands that seem too important to ignore. In these stressful modern times, almost everyone has days that seem to be ruled by crises or emergencies.

The second attention diverter is a frequent impulse to say or do something that seems justifiable in the moment. In those instances, simply because we can rationalize it, we settle for something less than our best.

See if you can remember personal examples from the past twenty-four hours—instances in which diversions or detours took you away from your most deeply held values and your best self. This exercise isn't meant to make you feel guilty. It's merely a matter of seeing just how commonplace is the process that Cayce described.

Of course, merely recognizing this aspect of the psychology of ideals still leaves unanswered one vital question: "What is the best ideal for us to hold?" Clearly the Cayce philosophy has in mind a specific spiritual ideal as the optimum: the universal Christ consciousness. It was demonstrated and lived by

Jesus, and its essence can be found in the other great faith traditions of the world. Just as significantly, it's a seed pattern in each one of us, no matter what faith tradition we may be following. It's a pattern of oneness—of interconnectedness and profound relationship.

Of course, many people aren't ready to make a commitment to the universal Christ consciousness (or even to a concept with similar wording to which they can better relate). For many individuals, that seems like too much to bite off, too big a stretch. Instead they would prefer to select an ideal that seems more within reach, although still demanding of them an effort to grow and change. Perhaps an ideal such as loving-kindness or peaceful centeredness or fairness would be more appropriate for now. Later in this chapter we'll examine one way in which you can decide for yourself on the best spiritual ideal to which you can make a commitment. Perhaps you'll choose the optimal ideal Cayce encouraged, or you may select something that is a more modest stepping-stone, eventually leading you to Cayce's optimum.

What happens in us when we make a commitment and invest ourselves in a personal spiritual ideal? The setting of a core value engages forces in the unconscious mind that can dramatically alter our lives. That's exactly why Cayce called it the most important experience that a soul can have.

But precisely what does it mean to set a spiritual ideal? Is it just a matter of telling someone else what you've done, or of writing it down on a piece of paper? Two crucial elements are central to the psychology of ideals. Both play a role whereby the forces of soul, lying dormant in the unconscious mind, are stirred to life. Both involve an act of free will and an engagement of the creative mind.

Aspiration is the first ingredient in Cayce's psychology of ideals. To hold the universal Christ as a spiritual ideal means to aspire to its qualities. Maybe those qualities seem out of reach, but we can feel ourselves inwardly stretching and reaching for all that the Christ consciousness means to us. The same would hold true for any other spiritual ideal chosen. What's most important to understanding the psychology of ideals is that the striving involves both the will and the creative side of the mind. We have to make the choice, and we need to use the imaginative forces to shape a relationship to that possibility for ourselves.

It probably comes as no surprise that aspiration is one of the two key ingredients in Cayce's view of how ideals work. Just think about how people use the word *ideal* in everyday language. It usually has the flavor of aspiration. For example, the ideal home situation is something that we can creatively imagine as the very best possible way of getting along with our family members. The ideal job is an imagined workplace situation that we long to have because all of our talents would be used.

Trust is the second ingredient in Cayce's psychology of ideals. It's a more subtle factor than aspiration. Think about how you might aspire to something but not trust that it's really alive within you, not trust that it's possible to experience for yourself. Without investing yourself through trust, you haven't yet set a spiritual ideal.

This may not be a point of view that's easy to swallow,

simply because most of us find trusting to be very difficult. To trust requires a more challenging use of free will than does aspiration alone. Trust means a willingness to surrender and let go of fears and doubts. It means placing ultimate belief in forces beyond our personal, conscious selves. According to this perspective, we haven't yet set the universal Christ—or anything else—as our spiritual ideal until we let go and put our trust in it.

Think about a somewhat superficial example—one that allows a quick remembrance of what it feels like to trust. When you turn on a light, you trust that the electricity will be there, ready to light up the room. When you turn the handle on the faucet, you trust that the water will start flowing. In other words, you spend little of your day worrying about the availability of power and water. Now, of course, a critic could say that you're mindlessly taking it all for granted—that many people in the world don't have immediate access to these resources, and that is certainly true. But the point of this analogy isn't how fortunate we are, but rather the way in which it is possible to trust something so much that it's foundational to how we think and act. These examples teach us something about trust—something that's related to *trusting an ideal* rather than the utility company.

The authentic ideal you hold is the one you don't have to spend time thinking about or questioning. It has become so much a part of your life that it's a given. When you meet a difficulty or a challenge, you know you can count on the inspiration and power of that ideal just as surely as you count on electricity and water if you are fortunate enough to live in a place where these physical resources are readily available. Some days your genuine ideal has the quality of being almost invisible to you because it's so deeply a part of how you look at the world. It's so essential that you don't stop to question it or worry about it.

Today's twenty-first-century world is an era that deeply needs a renewed vision of the power of ideals. Not pie-in-the-sky idealism—that too often fails to make the connection with practical life. What's so badly required in today's world is respect (even reverence) for that crucial step called "setting an ideal for one's own individual life." Cayce's spiritual psychology offers one very effective way to home in on exactly how to do it and make it work. Vivid aspiration is one key; the other is the courage to trust.

Getting in Touch with Your Individuality and Setting a Spiritual Ideal

Is your "individuality self" real to you, a part of your direct experience? Or does all this talk of a Higher Self, Real I, or "imprisoned splendor" sound nice but remain abstract theory? If it's only speculation you wish were true, then doubts will always creep in.

Maybe you know your individuality better than you think you do. Most likely you have caught glimpses of your Higher Ego on a fairly regular basis and may never have realized exactly what it was you were experiencing. It's probably safe to assume almost everyone has had direct encounters, however fleeting, with the Higher Self. Two methods are most common: seeing the qualities of your own individuality mirrored in other people whom you admire, and experiencing peak spiritual moments.

Perhaps it sounds strange that we could recognize our own spiritual nature in someone else. Doesn't the emphasis on "going within" and "exploring our own inner depths" deny the value of looking to other people? Maybe not. Could it be that we are psychologically built in such a way that the outer world often reflects the inner one?

You're probably familiar with this concept in regard to character faults. It's often been said that the shortcomings in other people that irritate you most are ones you have within yourself. This is called projection: You notice in the world around you those things that are in your own makeup. The notion probably makes you uncomfortable. You might try to squirm out of it by thinking of exceptions to the rule, but it's inescapably true.

If we'll admit projection happens, we can claim the good news too. Not only do we unconsciously project our faults onto others; we do the same thing with our good qualities. The excellence and virtue we see in those whom we admire are qualities of our own Higher Self.

Take a minute to think about this in a personal way. Make a note of several people whom you hold in great esteem. Pick at least one man and one woman. Then for each person you've selected, write down the positive qualities you see in that individual. Wait to read on until you've finished this task.

Now look at your list of qualities. It's impressive, isn't it?

Perhaps there is no one person living today who actively expresses all those attributes. Nevertheless, all those qualities exist within you as potential; otherwise you wouldn't be able to recognize them in other people. Admittedly, in a single lifetime you may not ever get around to developing all the potential of your individuality self. However, it's inspiring and hopeful just to imagine these virtues live in you.

The insights that come once you accept and work with positive projection provide one kind of clue about the nature of your Higher Self. Equally important is the revelation that comes from peak experiences. The word *revelation* is appropriate here, even though you may have never thought of yourself as a visionary or spiritual seer. Yet with a careful review of your life, you're sure to remember some extraordinary moments in which you caught the bigger picture of the meaning of life.

What are your peak spiritual experiences? Some of these moments may have come in childhood; others, in adolescence and adulthood. When have you felt intensely your Real I? One hint comes from the five aspects of the individuality self that were described earlier. Remember that each one ends with the letters *-ity*. *Unity* knows the oneness of all life. *Continuity* means that your essence is still developing, but it will live forever. *Sensitivity* perceives the visible and invisible realms. *Creativity* sees life with fresh, imaginative eyes. And *activity* means your Higher Self is involved with your daily life, whether you consciously experience it or not.

Peak spiritual moments that reflect the qualities of the Higher Self come in both ordinary and exceptional ways. Walking in nature, weeding a garden, or taking a quiet moment to love someone can suddenly turn into a revelation. Unexpectedly the familiar personality patterns of thinking and feeling disappear, and you reconnect with another side of yourself. Other times, a revelation of your individuality self can come in an extraordinarily encouraging dream that stays with you for weeks afterward. Or, on another occasion, a profound prayer and meditation experience can be the source of a peak moment.

The new identity is totally positive and uplifting, yet paradoxically, it feels both foreign and completely familiar. You're largely unacquainted with this mysterious part of yourself because you're in touch with it so rarely. However, it gives you the feeling of coming home to your true identity.

Take a moment now to think about your own peak moments. Spend some time reviewing your life from earliest childhood memories right up to the present. What are the experiences that stand out as spiritual high points? Some of these moments probably came in ordinary settings, but you perceived or understood what was going on in an exceptional way. Other times you may have been in an altered state of consciousness, such as a dream, hypnosis, or meditation. Many of these experiences will feel like they came as a gift to you—they can't be explained by anything you did to make them happen.

As you review your life and remember glimpses of your individuality self, re-create the experiences within yourself. Don't just remember what happened; let yourself relive in your imagination some of those moments with the same feelings, thoughts, and understanding. Wait to read on until you've finished this life review.

Now you're ready to summarize what you've seen about your Higher Self. Combine the understanding that comes from identifying with your positive projections and from re-living peak spiritual moments. Get as clear an image as you can of this place within yourself that is removed from your personality wheel. It's another center of personal identity. Even though you may have been in touch with it only on rare occasions, you know it's real. You may not know how to go back to it whenever you want, but there's no doubt in your mind it's authentic.

Next, give it a name or a label. Choose words that define or describe that place within yourself, as you best know it so far. Create a phrase that is personally meaningful because it captures the essence of your individuality center as you have experienced it. Here are some examples others have written:

- oneness of all life
- servant of Jesus
- boundless energy and love
- joyful trust

They aren't the "right" answer because there is no right or wrong in something like this. The words that ring true for you are the best ones.

Take some time now to formulate your own wording. Keep in mind that what you create is a temporary description. In the months and years ahead you will have further experiences of your individuality. As you do, your understanding will deepen and a different descriptive label may occur to you.

Once you've finished this task you may wonder what you've actually done. Have you defined the way you ought to be all the time? Have you specified your mission in life? Neither is true. No one can expect to be constantly in touch with his or her individuality center. Perhaps you can come to know it so clearly that it can guide important decision making and provide daily inspiration. However, it's foolish to put unrealistic pressure on yourself. You won't always measure up to the very best, but at the same time, it's important to define just what is the best you know.

The Cayce readings call such a personal standard the *spiritual ideal*. You have, in effect, set a personal spiritual ideal by choosing words to describe your individuality identity. This step is so vital that it is recommended in most of Cayce's more than nineteen hundred life readings. In helping people find purpose in life, he wisely counseled them in a systematic program for self-discovery. Often in the opening passages of a life reading, Cayce placed great emphasis on the importance of setting a spiritual ideal. In one reading this process of identifying and labeling the individuality self is called the "most important experience" that a soul can have in material life. The point of choosing a spiritual ideal is not to create a source of guilt for continual shortcomings. Instead it's a method of claiming the truth about yourself and aiming you in the right direction.

How does the wording of your spiritual ideal relate to your mission in life? The two are not identical because your spiritual mission for this lifetime involves specific tasks and service. However, the knowledge of your highest purpose in life resides in your individuality self. And the actual living of your mission—as distinct from merely knowing what it is—requires that your Real I harness the talents of your personality and direct its many I's. The clearer you are about the qualities of your real self, the more likely you are to be successful. In other words, when you choose a descriptive label for your individuality—when you set a spiritual ideal—you recognize the place in yourself that can guide all the further steps for finding and living your mission.

Of course, having a word or phrase to describe your spiritual ideal is really just one of the preliminary steps that lead to identifying your mission statement. No matter what quality, word, or phrase you choose for your spiritual ideal—love, Christ consciousness, Buddha, oneness with the Divine, peace, freedom—it should describe a place in you that you *know is possible* because of your peak spiritual moments.

What's more, the spiritual ideal becomes a beacon to your consciousness as you move into the myriad dimensions of the soul mind. *It designates the place within yourself from which you want to live your calling, whatever that mission may be.* The ideal designates the level of consciousness from which we invite a guiding spirit to reveal itself. In addition, that spiritual ideal begins to serve as a standard or measuring rod against which you can evaluate information that comes from your intuition, your dreams, and any other form of inner or outer guidance. Truly, without an ideal, we're like a ship without a rudder. But with a clear sense of a spiritual ideal, we are ready to move forward and prepare to receive and follow a calling in life.

CHAPTER 4

Faith and the Experience of a Call

Create in me a pure heart, O God. Open Thou my heart to the faith Thou hast implanted in all that seek Thy face. Help Thou mine unbelief in my God, in my neighbor, in myself. (262-13)

WHEN WE HEAR the word *faith*, we're likely to equate it with belief, especially in regard to matters of the soul and spirituality. However, in Cayce's psychology of the soul, there is an important distinction to be made, and that distinction underscores just how important faith is to our experience of a "call" and soul purpose.

Beliefs are tenets that we hold as truths. And so you might believe that there is a spiritual world and that something about us survives physical death. Faith, on the other hand (at least in the way Cayce invited us to understand it), is the actual experience of the unseen world. It is a knowing that does not depend upon supposition or outside authority. Faith is rooted in experiential insight.

In a similar way we could make a distinction between (1) figuring out what our mission in life probably should entail; and (2) directly experiencing a call. The first stays largely at the level of the intellectual mind, whereas the second is intuitive and heart-centered. From the *A Search for God* lesson sequence, the meditative affirmation for the fourth step—Faith—invites us to the second option. As you can see in the Cayce quotation that opens this chapter, the affirmation expresses the longing for heart consciousness that is pure. It affirms that something has already been placed within us, something that can be intuitively perceived and known directly. That "something" is faith itself, but it's also one's calling and soul purpose. In Cayce's psychology of the soul, one's life mission is imprinted within the unconscious mind as one comes into physical life. What's needed is a purity of intention and a willingness to trust one's capacity to "hear" a call and directly experience the nature of a mission.

One book that beautifully illustrates this human capacity for faith and the direct experience of soul purpose is Gregg Levoy's *Callings: Finding and Following an Authentic Life*. Working as an investigative reporter, Levoy traveled widely to interview people who felt they had experienced inner and outer guidance toward true vocation—"vocation" in the deepest meaning of its Latin root word *vocare*, meaning "to call." And so, rather than examine the lives of people who were happy or successful in their occupations, he investigated the lives of those whose stories had the extra dimension of feeling called by something bigger than themselves.

Levoy found that people had experienced their call in a variety of ways. Sometimes it was a set of synchronistic occurrences. For other people the call came through a profound prayer experience or a life-changing dream. There is almost endless variety in the stories his book recounts. But what the anecdotes have in common is the unshakable faith that was cultivated by these revelatory experiences. In each case, the individual had a direct experience of "something more" about life. There was a knowing that had been awakened. And that's what you want to strive for in your own journey to discover and live your soul's purpose. The work in this chapter in particular needs to be an exploration that is based on heart-centered, intuitive consciousness that builds upon the more analytical work we've done in the previous chapters.

A Personal Mission

Cayce's psychology of the soul starts with this premise: You have a mission in life. It's a magnificent adventure to discover that mission and live it. If you are like most people, the discovery process will take time. Little by little you will see the exact nature of your spiritual destiny. The discovery is similar to turning on a lightbulb that is connected to a dimmer switch. Instead of the bulb coming on fully in one instant, there is a gradual increase in light. Step by step the intensity grows. In the same way, you're likely to discover in increments your mission in life. Over months—perhaps over years—you'll see more clearly the characteristics of your soul's purpose.

It's a sad fact that in the modern world most people never find their life's purpose. Some people who fail to do so are very successful by worldly standards. They have money, power, and prestige, but they aren't really happy. Something deep inside them is dissatisfied and restless. They may try to ignore or hide this feeling, but often that leads only to illness.

Other people fail to find their mission because they get caught up in agendas that have little to do with their real calling. Their own busyness becomes the obstacle because there is no time for a spiritual search. The hectic, overcommitted quality of modern life is increasing in today's society, a trend that began to come into focus in the 1970s and 1980s. In 1988 respected pollster Louis Harris reported that in research conducted over the previous fourteen years there had been a drop of 36 percent in free-time hours for the typical American. As he put it, "The competition for time is getting fierce."* And with the rise of smartphones and other electronics technology, the pulls on our time and attention have only increased in the twenty-first century. We can conclude that if we really want to discover our soul's purpose, *the quest will have to be a priority.*

Already you've taken some big steps toward clarifying the characteristics of your mission: practicing self-observation, choosing a descriptive label for your individuality self, and identifying key talents and abilities. The work you've done in previous chapters has set the stage for what you can do now. You're ready to formulate a wording for your life's mission theme.

Remember in the Cayce readings a person's mission was

---

* Rick Lyman, "Leisure Crunch Gives Short Shrift to Culture," *Orlando Sentinel*, March 28, 1988. Downloaded from http://articles.orlandosentinel.com/1988-03-28 /lifestyle/0030050257_1_louis-harris-leisure-attendance.

not presented as a job title or single occupation. Instead it was portrayed in broader terms, as a direction for life. That mission statement always left room for many different career possibilities as well as free-time interests and volunteer activities.

For some people the mission is fulfilled most directly through the work they do. For others, their job is principally a way to earn money to pay the bills. Only in small ways do they find a chance to accomplish some aspect of their mission at work. People in this second category have to look outside the typical nine-to-five workday for activities that relate to a deep, spiritual calling.

What does a life mission statement look like? It defines the purpose of the soul in terms of talents and service. Here are three examples:

1. To be a spiritual leader using the arts as a way of reaching people
2. To help and guide others to see the spiritual meaning in numbers
3. To edit and reshape the ideas of others so those ideas can better be understood

This third example is an interesting case from the Cayce files. A woman in her sixties wrote and asked for a life reading. She was near retirement age but still had a strong curiosity to know the highest calling and purpose of her life. In her reading Cayce revealed the exact nature of her mission. Her true vocation was to act as a bridge between the masses of

people and those creative thinkers who couldn't always communicate their ideas very well. Her gift was with words and
their meanings. She was sensitive to what was and wasn't
clear to general readers.

This case is noteworthy because of what Cayce didn't say
to a person of this age. No references can be found to missed
opportunity. Nowhere in this reading is she criticized or con-
soled for having failed so far in her mission. Instead the tone
is one of promise and optimism. She is told that there is still
plenty of time to get on with the spiritual purpose for which
she was born. She isn't to be concerned about the past. Even
if she had floundered about for many years, at the time the
reading was given she still had the chance to harmonize with
her destiny.

These statements are equally true for anyone living today.
No matter how old you are, no matter how little you may have
seen or applied your soul's purpose until now, opportunities
still exist to get on track with your calling. Of course the ways
in which you act upon your mission at age thirty may be different from what you would do at age fifty or eighty. However,
be assured that at any point in your life there are things you
can do that relate to your highest purpose as a soul.

The same point was made in a reading given for another
woman. She wondered if she had any opportunities to fulfill
her mission and asked, "Is there anything in particular I can
do now to accomplish the reason for the present incarnation?"
Cayce's answer was both humorous and wise. He responded,
"If there hadn't been, you wouldn't be allowed to be in the

earth in the present" (3051-7). The same principle holds true for all of us today. We are here because we still have things to do in order to fulfill our missions.

Destiny and Free Will

Destiny is a word with several meanings and connotations, one of which is equivalent to the mission in life. Destiny implies that you were born with a plan. Even from birth certain patterns and forces were at work to guide your life along particular paths.

Any consideration of destiny invariably raises the question of free will. How can there be both a plan for your life and the freedom to be whatever you want? The solution to this philosophical dilemma begins with the recognition that destiny is not the opposite of freedom. The denial of freedom is predeterminism.

The Cayce readings, while they support the notion of destiny, clearly state that life is not predetermined. For example, one man asked in his reading about the accuracy of a prediction made by a psychic using mediumship. The medium had forecast that the man was sure to meet soon a wealthy individual who would support his career. Now the man wondered if this advantageous event was predetermined. Cayce answered that the future depended on the free will of the questioner. Certain opportunities were likely to come, but he had the freedom of his will in deciding how to respond to them.

In another reading, Cayce made the same argument in a more poetic way: "It is not that the entire life experience is laid out for an individual when there has been received that imprint as of the first breath . . . Choice is left to the individual" (281-49).

How far does destiny go in shaping the circumstances of life? Perhaps we can best understand the forces of destiny as a middle ground between free will and predetermination. Destiny implies your soul made choices in the distant past—or maybe just before your birth—and those choices make it very likely that certain people and events will come into your life. However, there is still room for you to maneuver. How will you react to those situations? What new things can you create out of the opportunities they give you?

You may have been destined to meet certain individuals in your life—for example, the person who is now your spouse or your boss. Nevertheless, destiny went only so far as your meeting. Ever since you encountered that soul with whom you have a destiny, the two of you have had the freedom to create what you will out of the situation. The quality of the relationship was not predetermined; it's the result of attitudes, feelings, and actions that each of you has freely chosen. Unfortunately the freedom of your will often goes unused. If your life is controlled by the automatic pilot of your personality wheel, old habits probably took over in the relationship. However, it didn't have to be that way, because no outside force predetermines your life.

Freedom and destiny also become an issue when we look

for signs in the material world. Can astrology, numerology, or palmistry indicate your mission in life? Cayce was asked this question on several occasions. In one reading he responded that astrology might be helpful to as much as 80 percent of the population when it comes to making career choices. In this case, astrology would be used as only one of many different tools in making a final decision.

In other readings, however, we can find stronger statements about the power of free will over astrological influences. Replying to one questioner, Cayce offered an arithmetical formula. Here again the figure of 80 percent came up, but this time in a different context. About 20 percent of the influences in our lives can be measured by esoteric arts such as astrology, numerology, and palmistry. The other 80 percent exists within the realm of our free will. If we make use of this freedom, it's stronger than any other influence that can be symbolized by planets, numbers, or lines on the hand.

Keeping the Right Attitudes in Your Search

Proper attitudes can help you start recognizing the specific nature of your soul's purpose. The best state of mind is a combination of three attitudes: patience, peace, and hope. They protect you from a malady that is suffered by many sincere seekers. It's a kind of tense desperation that worries, "I've just got to find my mission in life or else I'll ruin everything!"

The words may have come out differently in your own

mind, but have you ever felt this way? Does your honest desire to know the next step in your soul's journey ever turn
into a compulsive drive for achievement or a fear of failure? If
so, don't be discouraged. You aren't alone in that feeling.
Nevertheless, this kind of worry, compulsion, or fear doesn't
lead to the discovery of your mission.

The remedy is to start with patience, peace, and hope.
Patience—an active patience that is involved in things—
understands that life is long. It sees that every little moment
counts, but more important it knows the continuity of the
soul's life.

Peace creates acceptance. It allows you to see that the situations and events around you are happening for a purpose.
However, peace doesn't foster smugness or self-satisfaction. As
the Cayce readings often put it, "Be content but not satisfied."

Hope is the opposite of doubt. It affirms an orderliness to
the universe even when things outwardly appear to be random or chaotic. Hope makes trust—in God and in your own
Higher Self—possible.

If you can frequently maintain a state of mind that combines these three attitudes—patience, peace, and hope—
you're likely to make an important discovery. Not only are
you searching for your mission in life; your mission is searching for you. In other words the pursuit of your soul's purpose
has both active and receptive elements. On the one hand are
things you can do to discover the exact nature of your mission. On the other hand are the overtures for which you can
listen and watch.

Your individuality self, which is so often unconscious to

you, is always active. It leads you into situations and directs you to certain people. It provides hunches, intuitions, and quiet prompts. This deeper and more authentic self knows your highest purpose. It is ready and able to fulfill that mission. The entire burden of discovering your soul's purpose doesn't rest with your conscious, personality self. Help is frequently available because the mission is actively seeking you. No doubt there are important steps you must take, but don't forget to listen and be receptive too.

How Many Missions Do You Have?

Are you a busy person whose life is full of responsibilities and demands? Is almost every day packed with multiple tasks and challenges? If so, then the idea of a solitary mission may seem foreign. You might expect boredom if your life is focused on just one spiritual task. Since you are already accustomed to juggling several balls daily, why not take on many soul purposes? After all, more spiritual growth can be accomplished that way, right?

The Cayce life readings shed some light on this riddle. First, we should keep in mind that ultimately we all have only one purpose in life. It can be stated in a variety of ways, but it is essentially the same:

- To bring love consciously into the physical world
- To make the infinite finite
- To know ourselves to be ourselves, yet one with God

Second, the Cayce readings propose that each soul chooses just before birth a customized and specific mission that relates to the universal purpose. It's customized because it fits the needs and the abilities of that soul; it's specific because it focuses on certain ways of serving and creating.

However, you have many meaningful experiences that don't exactly conform to your mission statement. There are many supplemental opportunities to serve and create throughout your life. As an analogy, consider what happens if you marry. You make a commitment to love a particular man or woman, but marriage doesn't eliminate relationships with others. There are many ways of lovingly interacting with people that are not romantic. For example, a woman may be devoted to her husband and still love other men. The way she expresses her love and caring to the other men will be different from that to her husband, but marriage doesn't necessarily cut off other ways of reaching out. In the same way, the mission you have chosen as a soul is not the only way you will serve and create in the world during your lifetime. There are likely to be many additional approaches.

So your life will probably continue with many balls to be juggled. The Cayce readings suggest that some of the issues have to do with karmic problems you're trying to overcome in this lifetime. Other focal points involve new talents you're attempting to develop for later in this lifetime—and for those willing to entertain the concept of reincarnation, perhaps to develop in another incarnation. And yet, in the analogy of juggling, one ball corresponds to your mission in life. Finding your soul's purpose doesn't mean that you drop all the other balls and keep just one in the air. Certain balls may take on a special importance—you might want to toss them up a little higher than the rest—but all of them are meaningful experiences for you.

This conclusion leaves another problem unanswered. Can a soul's purpose change in the midst of one lifetime? Do we ever fulfill a mission before one life ends and therefore qualify to take on a new one? This is a genuine possibility. From a spiritual angle life is continuous and so the milestones we call birth and death are somewhat arbitrary. There is no reason why a mission couldn't extend well beyond one lifetime—or, for that matter, be fulfilled in less than one lifetime and prepare the soul to take on a new direction.

We must be careful, however, on this point. We may prematurely decide that we want to try something new. For example, when things are tough, it's easy to look for excuses. When the challenges are especially difficult, we may be tempted to say, "I'm ready to find my next mission in life."

Success also may lead to restlessness. When you're good at something for a long time, you may get bored. Then you face a question: Have you fulfilled one mission and do you now stand ready for the next one, or is it time to find new groups of people to touch with that same mission? For example, suppose a woman discovered early in her adult years that her soul's purpose was to be a channel for healing through words. For twenty years she worked successfully as a nurse. Her loving, supportive comments to patients were often the best medicine they received. She always seemed to know just the right thing to say to give courage or hope to someone struggling to regain health. However, she now feels restless and wonders if she's ready for a new mission. Perhaps she is, but first she should explore different ways to be a channel for healing through words. Does she have a gift for story writing or poetry, through which healing words can touch a new audience? Might the next phase of her mission involve counseling or teaching?

Each of us has one central purpose at any point in life, although other forms of outreach and creativity exist alongside it as a supplement. Most people retain that same central purpose throughout their lives. Nevertheless, a time may come when you can honestly say you have started into an entirely new phase of your life. It's conceivable that one day you'll discover your mission theme has changed. Suddenly a different set of talents and abilities seem to surface. A new set of opportunities and a different sense of yourself begin to emerge. At that point you are ready to discover anew your mission for the years ahead.

Preliminary Exercises for Finding a Mission Theme

How can you move from a list of your key talents and strengths to a succinct wording for your mission theme? It would be nice to have someone like Edgar Cayce to do this clairvoyantly for you, as he did for many people in their life readings. One thirty-five-year-old man was told that his most important strengths were intelligence, public speaking, and an ability to analyze people, circumstances, and purposes. His life reading from Cayce indicated that his mission was to be involved in diplomatic or economic relations among the nations.

A forty-year-old woman was told her special abilities included psychic sensitivity, the love of beauty, skill in working with her hands, and an appreciation for nature. She was encouraged to find meaning for her life through giving expression to the glories of nature and God.

A fifty-year-old woman was clairvoyantly examined by Cayce and described as a soul who had these special assets: writing, the ability to analyze accurately, an understanding of spiritual law, and abilities to instruct and direct others. Her reading concluded that these talents could best be harnessed through a life's purpose of helping people to find their right vocation.

However, on many occasions the Cayce readings did not reveal the precise wording of the individual's mission theme. That task was left to each person. There was probably great wisdom in that approach. Some people are more likely to fulfill their mission if they first have to search for it.

Several exercises will help you along that same path. First you'll pursue some preliminary methods that may give you clues or pieces of the overall puzzle. Later you can combine these insights during a final exercise that will lead you to a "first draft" wording for your soul's purpose. As you proceed through the five preliminary exercises, remember that some of them will probably work better for you than others. Make notes along the way, but expect that one or more of the exercises might not yield many useful results for you. Each exercise should be done with a playful, exploratory spirit.

Exercise 1. Take a few minutes to review your biography. Imagine a timeline that records every experience of your life up until now. As you look back, notice events and activities that created a special feeling for you at the time they happened. They are experiences that made you think to yourself or even say aloud, "This is the real me coming through as I do this. I need to be doing things like this more often." They are probably moments in which you engaged yourself fully in what you were doing, experiences in which you felt in sync with what was right for you to do at that time in your life. Modern psychology calls this Flow.

As a few of those memories come to mind, notice both what you were doing as well as *why* and *how* you were doing it. Sometimes the purpose for the activity or the spirit in which you did it can be the most important thing.

Jot down on a piece of paper the events from your past that fit this criterion. What does your list look like? You may get a clue about your mission in life by recognizing a pattern among some of the entries on your list. Do several of them draw upon the same talent or involve interactions with similar types of people?

Of course you can't jump to the conclusion that what you were doing in these special moments is exactly your soul's purpose. For example, one man wrote on his list the one-month hike along the Appalachian Trail he took after graduating from college. He can't necessarily conclude that his mission in life is to be an explorer or a park ranger. However, there may have been something crucial for him about that experience years ago. Maybe it was the spirit of adventure—something he'll need to recapture in order to now see his mission in life. Or perhaps it was the way in which he got in touch with his physical body.

Exercise 2. What is your fantasy of an ideal day? Although it can be fun to imagine the perfect vacation day that would get you reenergized, that's not the point of this exercise. Instead, envision an ideal day in the midst of responsibilities and involvement with people. Include events and activities that are especially meaningful for you.

This exercise is most valuable if you include lots of details. What time in the morning would you get up? What would you eat for breakfast? What would you do in the morning? And so forth. For the purpose of this exercise, don't limit yourself to the constraints imposed by actual circumstances in your life now. Let your imagination have free rein. Let it create images of how you would make use of your key talents on such an ideal day.

Exercise 3. How do you want to be remembered after your death? What accomplishments, types of service, creativity, and character traits do you hope you'll be known for? This may sound like a frivolous question, particularly if you're young and still have many years of life ahead, but it can be a useful way of intuitively catching some clues about your purpose in life.

Take a piece of paper and write your own obituary as you hope it might read years from now. Assume that you will live to a ripe old age. Don't worry about the typical parts of an obituary such as survivors and funeral arrangements. Instead, focus on a description of what you had to offer in life—how people saw you and what you did.

Exercise 4. How can your talents best work together? Up until now all of the methods you've practiced in this book have dealt with your talents in a piecemeal fashion. Each ability, strength, skill, or aptitude has been treated as independent from any other. However, that's not the way you experience your talents. Each one lives in the context and environment of other abilities that color and shape it.

Think about the four key talents and abilities, which you selected earlier, in a new way. Imagine they are a team. Each member of the team works for the good of the whole, just like a sports team or an interdisciplinary healing team. The talents support and enhance each other. They combine in such a way that the whole is more than the sum of the parts.

Synergy is that inexplicable magic that happens when many parts interact in a cooperative way to create something bigger than themselves. Your four key talents can work synergistically to fulfill your mission in life.

Take some time to think about your abilities in this way. See them as a team. What is that team equipped to do in life? For what is it especially well suited? This line of reasoning may give you some pieces of the puzzle about your mission.

Exercise 5. One of the best ways for many people to get clues about their missions is through guidance dreams. Sometimes a dream about your soul's purpose may come spontaneously. However, you don't have to wait for one. You can take steps to prepare yourself for this kind of help, by incubating a dream.

Dream incubation has a long history. The practice goes back at least to the dream temples of ancient Greece. Here people were readied to receive a dream related to the healing of some physical ailment. The dreamer hoped to be met by the god Aesculapius and to be given both diagnostic and prescriptive information. Temple priests played a role in the preliminary rituals and in the interpretation of the dreams.

In recent times dream researchers have reclaimed and adapted this basic procedure. The scope has been broadened to include most any kind of question. Of course, it still requires some skills in dream interpretation, but success has been achieved by many dreamers for a wide variety of problems. Guidance concerning your mission in life is one area you can easily explore.

The technique is simple and direct. What makes the method work is the sincerity of your desire to receive guidance. Choose a night when there is a good chance of your sleeping well. It's particularly helpful if you won't be aroused by an alarm but can instead waken gradually, maybe on a weekend morning. That one difference can make it much easier to remember your dreams.

Before you go to bed on the night of your dream incubation, spend a few minutes on some preparatory written exercises. Write down the question so that it asks exactly what you want to know. The following three examples show how you can pose the question in an open-ended way or ask for feedback on your current understanding:

- What's the next step for me for discovering my soul's purpose?
- What is my mission in life?
- Is my mission to be a bridge between the religious and scientific worlds?

Next, spend some time writing down your conscious knowledge related to the question. Make a list of the facts or data already available to you concerning this issue. Write down your key talents and abilities. Make a notation about the clues you have previously seen. Finally, if your question is open-ended (that is, it can't be answered with a simple yes or no), write your best guess about the correct answer.

Before you go to sleep, spend a few minutes praying about your question. Use whatever form or method of prayer feels best to you. The purpose of this step is to stimulate your sincere feelings about your question. Dream incubation usually works best when your heart is fully invested in what you're doing.

Finally, as you are drifting off to sleep, hold in mind your question. It doesn't have to be the very last thing you think of before falling asleep, but try to keep some attention on the issue as you enter that halfway state called the hypnagogic level.

When you awaken—in the middle of the night or in the morning—write down any dreams you recall, whether or not they seem at first to be relevant. If you don't get any dreams the first night, try again a second or third time.

What is the meaning of the dreams you receive? Perhaps the best way to approach dream guidance is to see it as one of several inputs for your decision making. It's a supplement to other sources as you formulate a final answer. Rarely will a dream give you a reliable solution all by itself. Instead you are likely to find that dreams about your soul's purpose do one of three things: (1) fill in the gaps of your knowledge with missing information; (2) demonstrate possibilities you may want to explore in waking life; or (3) give you feedback on your current waking perspective.

What gaps in your knowledge might a dream fill? It could be a specific talent that you've ignored or left unrecognized. It might be a promising way to make use of some ability. Another kind of missing information relates to your personality wheel. Frequently a dream will symbolically show you an obstacle that thwarts your mission—some personality pattern that blocks your progress.

Dreams can also be a rehearsal stage. At night you sometimes try out possibilities. For example, a guidance dream might show you (or another dream character who actually represents an aspect of you) doing something that is a part of your soul's purpose. Remember the illustration of this principle given earlier: A stockbroker dreamed repeatedly that he was lecturing before large audiences on the subject of spiritual truth. This was both a reminder of a talent and a rehearsal of one expression of his mission. The dreams were a demonstration of an important possibility for him.

Finally, guidance dreams can give you feedback on the accuracy of your waking life understanding. They can confirm that you're on track or warn you that you're headed down a dead-end road. However, this function of your dream life can operate only if you first try to arrive at a conscious decision. The unconscious mind can then act through dream imagery to support or discourage your conscious mind's assessment.

For example, suppose you have worked with the previous four exercises to get some clues about your soul's purpose. You think that the pieces of the puzzle are beginning to fit together and that the wording for your mission theme is something like "helping the disadvantaged and forgotten to gain self-respect." That sounds admirable and it may nicely fit your talents, but is it correct? Is it actually what you were born to do? One way to get some feedback is to ask your dreams. Everyone's dream imagery is highly personal and varied, but actions and symbols that denote success or harmony probably are encouragement that you are on the right track. The possibilities are almost endless, but watch for confirming signs like these: arriving successfully at your destination, a musical instrument that is well tuned, or getting a good grade in school. At the same time look for dream images that suggest you are mistaken. It might come as a literal interpretation of a well-known phrase such as being caught off base in a baseball game or seeing a train that has slipped off its tracks. Or the negative feedback could show you getting lost in the dream or being misunderstood by those around you.

Obviously there are no infallible rules for working with dream guidance. However, when dreams are used in conjunction with other approaches, they can be a valuable addition. Dreams provide new insights from the unconscious side of yourself and frequently allow your individuality self to give you important clues for finding your mission in life.

Formulating Your Mission Statement

Using the clues and pieces of the puzzle obtained by the previous exercises, you're ready to create a succinct wording for your central mission in life. What you write down at this point is a best guess, a tentative statement based on the most promising insights you have gained so far. Later you may find that somewhat different wording is more appropriate, but for now you'll select words that capture your best understanding. It's a first draft.

You'll probably find it beneficial to look at some more examples. They can help to "prime the pump" of your own creativity. Sample mission statements show how other people have discovered ways of expressing their own souls' purposes. The wordings chosen by these individuals probably don't match exactly your own mission statement, but you may get some additional hints for how to go about conceiving your own.

Where do these prototypes come from? Some are taken directly from the Cayce readings. They are expressions offered in life readings for individuals who sought to find their purposes in life. Other examples are from contemporary people who have applied the steps outlined in this book and have found for themselves a statement of their missions.

Try this approach for getting the most out of the examples: First get yourself into a meditative frame of mind. Spend a couple of minutes sitting comfortably and letting your attention focus on the word or phrase descriptive of your individuality self—that is, the words you chose to define your spiritual ideal. Then spend a minute or two thinking about your four key talents and abilities. In your imagination feel yourself reaffirming and reclaiming them.

At this point you'll be ready to get the most from the example mission statements listed next. Spend approximately twenty to thirty seconds thinking about each one. As you focus on a specific sample statement, pretend that this really is your purpose in life—"try it on," so to speak. Visualize yourself living with this mission. Follow the same imaginative steps you might use if you were looking to buy a house. When you visit a house that is on the market, you're likely to walk through it trying to visualize what it would be like to live in that house. In a similar way, pretend for just a minute that the example mission statement is your own. How does it feel to you? Does it fit you? Would that mission in life draw upon your talents and abilities? Would you be fulfilled with this as your central purpose?

One by one consider all the sample statements with this method, and then you'll be ready to write your own. As you work with these examples, watch for little clues that will be useful: phrases with which you resonate or particular words that stand out for you. You may even find that one or two of the sample statements feel as if they are very close to the way you'll want to word your own.

SAMPLE MISSION STATEMENTS

- To appreciate and reflect beauty
- To magnify ideals and aspirations in myself and in others

- To be a unifier, one who synthesizes and blends the fragments of life
- To be an agent of inner and outer peace
- To innovate, to be one who gets new things started
- To be the discerning and wise analyst of life
- To attract and channel material supply
- To manifest God's love through the family
- To transmit and clarify new ideas
- To be a channel for healing through words
- To compassionately work for justice in the world
- To be a spokesperson for the truth
- To persuade and convince people to accept the best
- To be a catalyst for change in the world
- To be a planter of positive seeds in people's lives
- To promote freedom and its responsible use
- To conserve and be a good steward of resources
- To be a crusader for equality in the world
- To nurture new beginnings in individuals and groups
- To make mechanical things work better to serve people
- To adapt, complete, or decorate things to make them more useful and beautiful
- To be a creative, cooperative team member
- To direct and manage people to bring out their best
- To build new structures and organizations that help humanity
- To support and coach people overcoming disabilities
- To start and run responsibly new business enterprises to meet people's needs

In order to write a first-draft wording of your own mission statement, you may want to jot down initially some phrases or words that you'll want to include. If you find it difficult to craft your thematic statement all at once, such a preliminary step is probably a good idea. This method was used by the woman who ultimately wrote, "To compassionately work for justice in the world." At first she wrote down two fragments that she suspected would be parts of her final statement. She knew she wanted to incorporate the phrase "justice in the world" and she felt that her capacity for compassion was her most prominent talent. Once she had these two elements on her paper, she was able to arrive at a final wording for her first draft.

Spend some time on this task. You might even want to sleep on it for a night and then see what comes to mind in the morning. After you've come up with a wording that feels promising, you'll be ready for the next phase of our journey. Part II is all about practical application: testing the validity of the mission statement in daily life and finding ways to live your life with purposefulness.

PART II

Living
Your Soul's Purpose

*Q. Has she anything in particular to contribute to the world,
and in what direction?*

*A. Each soul that enters the material manifestation has some-
thing to contribute—even though it be merely the care of
others in every direction.* (1350-1)

*For, each soul enters with a mission. . . . we all have a mission
to perform.* (3003-1)

PART II OF this book is all about application. We'll explore
what it looks like and how it feels to live with a sense of mission and purpose guiding everything we do.

Application—putting promising ideas to the test—is central to the Cayce philosophy. He taught that in the application
comes the awareness. In other words, it's only through *acting*
on ideas that their real meaning can change one's consciousness.

Just as important is the way Cayce chose to name the
organization he founded and led. In 1928 when the first holistic hospital in America was opened in Virginia Beach, a

reading was given by Cayce in which a name was proposed: the Cayce Hospital for Research and Enlightenment. Right at the heart of this work is research—the attitude of experimenting and testing principles in one's own life. Even after the hospital was a financial failure and had to be closed, the new organization that was founded in 1931 to continue his work, the Association for Research and Enlightenment, still carried in its name that essential phrase.

And so, in that same spirit, part II invites you to be a *personal* researcher. The chapters that make up this section of the book are focused on practical application. It starts with chapter 5, in which you will put to the test the draft mission statement you wrote in the previous chapter.

The next chapter brings application right down to one of the most practical and physical aspects of living your life purpose: money. In chapter 6 we'll explore how financial issues relate to your mission, and we'll examine Cayce's approach to getting in harmony with the law of abundance.

Then, in chapter 7 we'll examine the question of how to find the right job. Even though one's soul purpose is bigger than just an occupational label, one's job is often a primary vehicle for living the mission. It can take a lot of time, energy, and experimentation to find just the right kind of work that allows your gifts to shine through. This final chapter offers some specific methods you can apply for finding the best fit.

CHAPTER 5

A Personal Research Project

YOU'VE WRITTEN A first-draft statement of your mission in life. It describes a theme that may be your central purpose as a soul for this lifetime. However, you probably wonder whether it's valid. It looks good and feels right. It would require you to make use of your key talents and abilities. But is it really what your individuality self intends to accomplish?

How could you get verification? It would be nice to have available an accurate sensitive like Edgar Cayce to make a definitive pronouncement. However, you may not be able to locate such a reliable clairvoyant. Or, if you did find one, maybe the expense of a reading or the waiting list makes that option unacceptable.

A better solution is to make your own efforts to validate your mission statement. You can become a spiritual researcher whose experimental laboratory is life itself. In fact, this is the approach that the Cayce readings usually recommend. A fundamental idea taken from this material asserts: In the application comes the awareness. In other words, authentic knowledge and understanding come only through practical efforts to apply ideas. Speculative knowledge is one thing. You can read books or listen to teachers to collect facts and theories, but you don't really know something until you've lived it!

Cayce felt so strongly about this point that he included the word *research* in the name of the organization based on his work—the Association for Research and Enlightenment (A.R.E.). Edgar Cayce's own organization, therefore, was envisioned as one whose most essential nature was research and application. The A.R.E. was founded in 1931, fourteen years before Cayce's death, and many readings were given about its inner workings. Those readings contain advice to its leaders about how to shape the programs and activities of the association. We can find several readings in which the importance of research is stressed. In one reading the leaders are chastised for trying to present the work as enlightenment without any research. They are warned that this is like "putting the cart before the horse." Spiritual growth doesn't operate that way.

This principle is just as true today as it was then. Enlightenment is not something you can get from collecting facts, even if that information concerns spiritual matters. Reliable truth that can feed your soul's hunger for meaning and purpose comes only from application. You must try living what you believe. And if those beliefs are valid, then you'll observe positive fruits from your practical efforts. These will be described in detail later in this chapter.

This spiritual law is the basis of your next step for discovering your soul's purpose. You have selected a likely possibility for your mission. It's promising because it fits many of the characteristics of mission statements given in Cayce life readings. Now you're ready to conduct some personal research to test its validity.

The Nature of Research

What is research? Many people are intimidated by the word because of its connotations: intellectual scientists, sterile laboratory garments, even a denial of the invisible, spiritual side of life. But we should distinguish between the neutral approach of science itself and the bias of *scientism* and its prejudices. Science is a method of open-mindedly seeking truth. Its approach, the scientific method, carries no bias about the nature of reality. Scientism, however, with its use of the scientific method, carries considerable baggage. By making strong assumptions about the nature of reality, it has a worldview that ignores the spiritual realm as well as related phenomena such as ESP.

In this chapter you are invited to use the scientific method, but you won't have to practice scientism. You'll follow the time-tested steps used by scientific researchers for hundreds of years. First comes a hypothesis, a theoretical best guess about something. Second comes the design of a practical way to test that hypothesis, followed by the application of that test. As the test proceeds, data is collected by careful observation.

Next, there is an evaluation of the information gleaned from the experiment. Finally, a conclusion is drawn to validate the hypothesis or to go back and revise it.

Getting Started on Your Research Project

Your hypothesis for the research project in this chapter is the notion that you have accurately written a statement for the mission in life that you as a soul selected just before birth. Now you need to design a practical way to test that hypothesis. Your next step is to come up with a game plan for putting this mission into action. As you apply that strategy, you can also become a careful observer and watch for results that verify or invalidate your hypothesis.

A game plan to experiment with a mission statement should have two sections. Anyone's authentic purpose has two ways in which it is meant to be lived. One involves touching the lives of other people in constructive ways; the other involves applying the mission in relation to oneself so that development of the individuality self takes place.

Service is a key part of living one's mission. Although it often makes us uncomfortable to hear this biblical line, the Cayce readings frequently remind anyone looking for the meaning of life that "we are our brother's and sister's keeper" (Genesis 4:9). And for those who are willing to consider the possibility of many lifetimes, the theory of reincarnation makes this no less true. Rebirth may help explain why people suffer as they do, but it doesn't absolve us of responsibility for helping people overcome their problems. What's even more hopeful, service can be fun! Reaching out to others doesn't have to be a duty that is begrudgingly undertaken. Here's one of the most amazing discoveries we can make: Creative, loving service to people and to the world at large is a joy.

The second method, the mission in relation to yourself, is easily overlooked. No doubt spiritual progression happens as a result of service to others, but there is also a component of the mission that should more directly focus on nurturing one's own Higher Self. Remember that the Higher Self is not yet fully evolved. It still needs development, but what distinguishes it from the personality or ordinary self is that the Higher Self is capable and willing to grow.

If you forget to live your soul's purpose in relation to yourself, then you're a prime candidate for burnout, a common feature in today's world. Burnout is often the experience of someone who is more or less on track with his mission but applies it in a one-sided way. All the emphasis is upon reaching out to others, and the need to balance things with self-nurturing activities is forgotten. This condition is usually the product of misunderstanding about selfishness.

Exactly what is selfishness? Can you invest time and energy in yourself without being selfish? The Cayce readings most clearly answer those questions in the reply to a playwright who asked if his manuscript had successfully made his intended point about the pitfalls of the self in the script. The response from Cayce was that he should distinguish in his own mind between the words *self* and *selfish*. Self is of God; selfish is of evil. In other words, God honors and respects the individuality of each one of us. However, we can distort the meaning of individuality and develop a willfulness toward private fulfillment, a preoccupation with personal concerns despite their effect on others. That becomes selfish and is not the path to genuine spiritual growth.

In another reading we can find the same idea: "Ye are to fulfill the purpose for which each soul enters the earth—which is to manifest to the glory of God and to the honor of self" (3333-1). This is a restatement of the universal purpose shared by all souls. The first part probably doesn't surprise you: We are here to glorify God. However, many people find the final five words of this passage—"to the honor of self"—difficult to interpret.

What does it mean to honor oneself? Consider some of the appropriate synonyms for *honor*: *appreciate*, *cherish*, *love*, *respect*, and *value*. If it's the individuality self toward which you hold these attitudes, then surely this is in keeping with what you were born to do. In fact, by honoring your Higher Self and investing time getting closer to it, you become more capable of living your mission in service to others.

Designing Your Experiment

To test your hypothetical mission statement, the one you wrote at the conclusion of the previous chapter, you can commit yourself to applying a series of steps pointed toward fulfilling the mission. The results of that practical application will give you reliable knowledge about its validity or error.

An experimental plan with small steps is usually better than one with big steps. Overly ambitious intentions often go unapplied. If your research project has several bite-size parts, you're more likely to do something with them.

As already described, some aspects of your plan will involve ways of reaching out to others in terms of your mission statement. For example, suppose your hypothetical purpose is worded "To be a unifier, one who synthesizes and blends the fragments of life." What are some little steps that you could take in order to test its validity? Maybe you'll volunteer to be an officer of your local civic league. You've noticed considerable differences of opinion on several current topics. Perhaps your talents and mission equip you to play an important service role among your neighbors. Or maybe you'd like to lead a study series at your church on the religions of the world. You may not be an expert on the topic, but you're open-minded. You're willing to see how diverse beliefs have points of commonality, and your leadership in such a study group could be very helpful to others. A third possibility for your research game plan could be tried at your job. This small step in application wouldn't involve the large and dramatic step of changing jobs. Instead, you might find new ways to be a unifier in your current professional setting. For example, you might commit yourself to assisting two fellow employees who never seem to get along. Maybe your gift for synthesizing and blending will help them find a way to unify their efforts at work.

However, these sample parts of a research plan are only half the story. The other half concerns how you can be a unifier to yourself. What are the fragments of your own life that need to be synthesized and blended? For example, if you've been so busy for years that you've lost touch with the playful side of yourself, maybe it's time you found a way to blend your identity with it occasionally. One small step you can take to reconnect with your playful side is to set aside an hour each week to do something that's simply fun without any judgment of its practicality.

Focusing on your talents is another approach for testing your mission statement in relation to yourself. Does one of your key talents, abilities, or strengths have room for improvement or expansion? Perhaps you imagine that teaching is a way you want to communicate your unifying, synthesizing vision. It is one of your natural aptitudes, but you know it could be even better. A small step toward fulfilling your mission could be to invest some time and money to take a training course for lecture and teaching skills.

All of these sample illustrations are highly speculative. Now you're ready to create your own research game plan. You may wonder how extensive a strategy you should develop. First create a lengthy list of possibilities. Later you'll commit to only two or three forms of outreach and two or three ways to nurture your best self.

One method to develop your list involves a look back at your sub-personalities. In chapter 2 you began to work on recognizing various I's that combine to make up your total personality. Some sub-personalities aren't particularly interested in your soul's purpose, and they may even offer strong resistance. However, other I's may be ready and capable of playing a role, especially if they receive direction from the individuality self.

Take a few minutes to review the I's in yourself that you have noticed. Could any of them contribute to your soul's purpose? Would any of them play a role in testing your mission statement? What are some small steps that could be part of your research strategy?

Another way to build your list of possibilities is to brainstorm with a friend. Tell that person what you are trying to accomplish and share the mission statement you've conceived. Remember that brainstorming means anything goes. Don't stop at this point to judge the ideas that you or your friend come up with. Just let the ideas fly, knowing that some of them will be ridiculous. Later you can look back over the list and pick just a few that seem worthy of your research efforts.

Research Projects of Three People

Let's return to the three case histories that were introduced in chapter 2. These individuals followed the same steps you've been working on, and they eventually arrived at tentative wordings for mission statements and game plans for application.

Kate, the twenty-four-year-old beautician, identified her four key talents as sensitivity, a sense of humor, a friendly nature, and an eye for beauty. She eventually arrived at a wording for her mission in life: "Helping people to get a new self-image." This intuitively felt right to her and was obviously a mission statement worth testing for its validity. She recognized how some situations from her past already indicated this might be her soul's purpose.

When she was a teenager, friends in distress always seemed to turn to her for help. She had a knack for assisting them to see themselves and their problems in a new way. As a young adult she found that this theme continued through her profession. Hairstyling gave her a very direct way of helping people to gain a new self-image. Virtually every day customers came to her because they wanted to start feeling differently about themselves. But at the same time, Kate could see that she had always been rather unconscious of what she was doing with her clients. She had taken pride in doing her job well, but hadn't been aware of the deeper impact that she was having on people.

When she set about writing down some specific exercises to test her mission statement, she began with outreach to others. The first item in her game plan for application was to start being more conscious of both the psychological and physical changes she was making in the lives of her clients. As she became more alert to the opportunities at hand, she was able to make even greater use of her playful humor and sensitivity with people, helping them shape new images of themselves.

A second item in this part of her application plan concerned interaction with her friends and family. She set a goal to point out more frequently the positive, yet easily forgotten, sides of these key people in her life. For example, she helped her younger brother gain a better self-image by reminding him on several occasions just how good he had been at artistic efforts when they were children, an aspect of himself that he had ignored for years.

A final item in the service part of Kate's game plan was to do volunteer work once a week at a local soup kitchen. These downtrodden homeless men and women were not the sort of people with whom Kate usually had much involvement. How could she help them to get a new self-image? If the tentative wording of her mission statement was accurate, its basic theme should have applicability in areas beyond her immediate occupation. She followed through on this part of her plan, and she discovered something surprising: In small ways that had nothing to do with styling hair, she had a natural gift for helping people to see themselves in a new way. There were no dramatic reversals in life situation for any of the people she met and talked to every Sunday evening. However, she saw in little ways that her encouraging words and insights were having an effect.

All of these activities involved just the first part of Kate's application plan: expression of the mission statement in service to others. Just as important was to live it in relation to herself. She needed to find ways to keep a fresh, positive self-image. Her first experiment was to get in touch more fully with the playful side of herself. She enrolled in a clowning workshop. It proved to be an effective way to use her talent for humor in order to overcome some inhibitions.

A second item in this part of her application plan was a commitment to explore an undeveloped aspect of herself. She enrolled in a noncredit course on computers, something that seemed alien to her in the mid-1980s world in which she was doing this personal experiment. She had always believed she was rather dumb when it came to mathematics or computer science. She procrastinated for a while before following through on this, and it eventually proved to be somewhat of a failure. She didn't enjoy the course and thought the instructor was insensitive to people without a natural talent for logical thinking. However, even though this part of her application plan wasn't successful, it didn't make her lose confidence in the reliability of her mission statement. Overall, her experiments reinforced the notion that she derived the greatest meaning from life by helping people to get a new self-image.

Rudy, the fifty-nine-year-old physician, selected as his four most significant talents leadership, teaching, planning, and courage. He finally arrived at the following wording for his soul's purpose: "To aid people or groups to get across an impasse." The image he formed of himself living this mission was Saint Christopher, the patron saint of travelers. Legend has it that Saint Christopher transported travelers across a stream, once carrying the Christ child himself. Without someone like this helper-servant, those on their journey would have found their way permanently blocked by the river.

Past experiences indicated that Rudy had a natural gift for this helper-servant role. He often worked with his patients in a holistic manner, viewing the illness as an impasse for the soul, not merely annoying symptoms to be eliminated with medication. Frequently and successfully he cared for patients, helping them mentally, emotionally, and spiritually through the impasses symbolized by their ailments. He had also lived this mission theme for several years through the private school that he founded. Even after he turned control of the school over to others, he had many opportunities to help that leadership group through one impasse or another.

Those previous successes were encouraging signs and had also influenced him to select the wording that he did for his mission statement. However, to validate this expression of his soul's purpose he needed to do more than merely look back, so he formulated a game plan to apply this theme in ways that would require new initiative.

In relation to others, Rudy made a commitment to develop new methods to use his abilities to teach and lead. He helped create and conduct a four-day educational conference designed for people who wanted to find their calling in life but felt blocked. His lectures and workshops largely focused on helping people through their impasses in order to find greater meaning in life. His mission statement was reinforced by the success of that program and the positive feedback he received from the seventy-five participants.

A second item in his application plan was to create a support group for people trying to identify their personal destinies—people who also were willing to encourage others in the process. His initial work with these people was productive; participants gained new insights about themselves. He assumed if he met with the group for three or four weeks, then they could continue without him. But the group appeared to break up once Rudy stopped meeting with them. To his surprise some members of the group sought him out several months later and expressed a strong interest in continuing their work together. What had seemed like only a partial success at best came to life again.

Rudy also formulated a plan to help himself with impasses in his own development. One aspect of this plan was to seek out mentally and spiritually healthy people who were perceptive and who would help him identify his own obstacles to growth. He also made a commitment to a support group, not as the leader but as a participant seeking help to overcome some of his own impasses. And finally, he set a goal to work with concentration and meditation exercises as a way of staying in touch with his individuality center.

Carol, the woman in her thirties with a wide variety of previous occupations, picked these four talents as her most important: writing, sensitivity to feelings, creativity, and an ability to see the big picture. She formulated the following wording for her mission statement: "To help people through transitions." Like the statements chosen by Kate and Rudy, Carol's relates to helping people (others and herself), but in this case it focuses on people who are going through some kind of life transition—a move, marriage, birth, death, career change, or any other major change.

Carol was able to see circumstances in her past in which she had already been successful in this role. Years earlier, when she was living in Alaska, she made several visits to British Columbia, Canada, to be with a friend who was going through three demanding transitions: the serious illness of her father, the loss of her home, and her own mental breakdown. On two of the three occasions Carol just happened to be there when her friend's crisis began. Only in the case of the mental breakdown did she intentionally plan to go and help out. However, in all three situations Carol was the key person helping her friend through these trials.

An event with her mother provided what is perhaps the best example from Carol's past in which she helped someone through a transition. She was called to stay with her mother while she recovered from a critical illness. This was an important opening for Carol because she had a great deal of anger and resentment toward her mother and had set a goal to resolve these feelings. Nursing her mother became the perfect way to heal those wounds. In a sense, Carol not only helped her mother through the transition of her illness, but she also helped herself through the transition of resolving emotional scars.

When it came time to look ahead and try to further validate the wording of her mission statement, Carol found it difficult to preplan interactions with people going through transitions, so her principal discipline was to be willing to serve in this way and stay on the lookout for opportunities. Many came to her in the months immediately after she had formulated a wording for her soul's purpose. Often the situations had a serendipitous quality to them.

At one point Carol had just finished directing a theater production and had recently met a writing deadline. She had no plans or work lined up to follow, something her husband considered very unbusinesslike and negligent. Then a call came from an out-of-town friend who needed assistance with the impending birth of her second child. As if to confirm the rightness of her going to help out, a sign appeared. The very day Carol went to buy her plane ticket for the trip, two checks arrived in the mail totaling the cost of the ticket (plus thirty cents).

On another occasion she had two free days before a new job was to start. Carol went to visit a friend who had been the source of many favors in the past. This friend was in a panic because the moving van was scheduled to arrive in two days and she had no experience packing a household. She could expect little help from her disabled husband and four grade-school-aged children. Carol took charge of organizing things and even had some time left over to throw a going-away celebration.

One important feature of the validation process stood out for Carol: the feeling of something bigger working through her in spite of personal intentions that were more selfish. She observed that in some situations she was initially motivated by curiosity or personal needs, only to find an unanticipated opportunity to fulfill her mission. Suddenly she would find herself engaged in a larger purpose than she had expected. Often she would see serendipity at work: looking for one thing and finding something else. In fact, she discovered that if she tried to force herself into a circumstance as someone's savior, she usually experienced unpleasant consequences. Success in her mission came most often through the unlikely coming together of people and situations.

Equally important was Carol's plan for helping herself through transition times. She could see from looking back at her life a tendency to do destructive things in the midst of transitions. Now she was prepared to define a more creative and balanced way to move through challenges. Her application plan included these four personal challenges:

1. Do focused, calming activities such as walking, gardening, intense work, or visiting with my wisest and most experienced friends.
2. Get some time alone. Separate myself for a while and tell people, "I'm having a hard time at the moment," so that my behavior, confusion, and isolation aren't perceived as rejection.
3. Read things that come to me unexpectedly, trusting that they may contain ideas that will help me through my transition.
4. Use affirmations to keep proper perspective on what's happening. For example: "This has to be gone through" or "This is a transition, not a permanent condition."

This four-part approach worked well for Carol when she used it to live her mission statement in relationship to herself. It didn't remove difficult transitions from her life. Some still took a long, exhausting time to pass, but she was able to move quickly and joyfully through others.

Overall, Carol had a similar experience to those of Kate and Rudy. Although not every part of their application plans was totally successful, they each gained greater certainty that they had correctly identified the life directions and missions for which they are especially gifted. The small-step efforts to experiment and take initiative with the mission theme supported its reliability and accuracy.

Evaluating the Results of Your Research

You've completed the first two steps that are part of any research project. First you formulated a hypothesis; in this case, a tentative statement of your soul's purpose. Next you designed a series of practical steps for testing your hypothesis. Now you're ready to start applying your game plan and experiment with the validity of your mission statement.

In the days and weeks that it may take to apply all the small-step tasks you have chosen, what should you look for? This is the period in which a scientist—including a spiritual scientist—collects data through careful observation. Later this information will be evaluated so that conclusions can be drawn.

But what kind of careful perception is needed? What measurements gauge whether you've successfully identified your true mission in life?

Obviously the criteria for success must fit the nature of the investigation. For example, remember how Thomas Edison conducted his research with possible filaments for an efficient electric lightbulb. Each new round of experimentation involved a revised hypothesis: Some different metal or alloy was the best one to use. What kinds of observations did he make each time he created a new version of his prototype lightbulb? Two qualities were most important: illumination and longevity. The filament had to burn brightly, and it had to last a long time before failing. It took him fourteen months of trial and error before he discovered the best answer.

When it comes to testing the validity of your mission statement, what qualities and characteristics are associated with a life that is fulfilling its deepest purpose? You're likely to observe some or all of the following seven experiences when you finally start living what you were born to do. As you apply your practical game plan, watch for them. They are signposts along the way—reinforcing, positive feedback that encourages you and validates your mission statement.

1. *A sense of wonder.* It's easy to fall into predictable routines, but on occasion you may have moments of wonder. These extraordinary experiences put you back in touch with the magic of living. They reunite you with your spiritual source. Unexpected new opportunities present themselves; awe-inspiring events surprise you. Windows that you never thought existed can open to new points of view. These moments may happen when you behold the majesty of nature or feel the soul of someone as you look deeply into his or her eyes. They can come as you awaken from a profound dream or when for no obvious reason you just feel glad to be alive.

   No doubt you've experienced a sense of wonder. Many of those memories may come from childhood because most individuals are more open and receptive in their youth than they are as adults. However, people of any age are candidates for a reconnection with the inner and outer magic of existence.

How often do you have moments of wonder? If the experience started happening more often in your life, would you notice it? Probably you would. In fact, this is one experience that is likely to become more frequent when you begin to fulfill the destiny for which you were born. It's one of the signposts indicating success.

Of course, you can hardly expect to carry on sixteen or eighteen hours a day deeply in touch with a sense of wonder. Even people who are living their souls' purposes still have days of being grouchy or ill. Actively working toward your mission in life doesn't eliminate the difficulties of coping with the modern world. But on a more frequent basis you may begin to catch a surprising, awe-inspiring glimpse of the special magic of life.

2. *Seeing others benefit from your efforts.* Everyone's mission involves some component of creative service to others. We're here to help each other. As one Cayce reading puts it: "Know that the purpose for which each soul enters a material experience is that it may be a light unto others" (641-6). For some individuals that means hands-on work such as social services, counseling, or medicine. However, just as valuable is the indirect service rendered by an artist or musician whose creations inspire, animate, and brighten our thoughts and feelings.

As you make careful observations and watch for this second characteristic, be sure to look beyond your occupation. Your job may bring benefits to others, but so can your outside interests, your hobbies, and your way of living. And as you see others being assisted and blessed by what you say and do, take it as confirmation that you are getting more in sync with your true calling.

3. *Feeling the presence of God.* When you express your soul's purpose, you will experience more often the reality of the Divine. However, this promise doesn't answer the question of exactly how you will feel that presence. If your expectations stay amorphous or beyond conception, it's unlikely that you'll recognize these extraordinary moments when they come. The presence of God is sometimes encountered in subtle ways and you can miss it unless you know what to look for.

For a moment, think about God with this definition: total wholeness and completion. Now ask yourself, "In what way do I most frequently detect my own lack of wholeness? How do I most directly experience my own failure to be complete?" Maybe you'll recognize this key factor as loneliness or as confusion. Perhaps you'll see that you aren't whole because you feel trapped and limited or because you're in a sort of symbolic darkness.

No matter what you observe, you now possess a way of anticipating how the presence of God will meet you. As the Tibetan Buddhist scholar Lama Anagarika Govinda has pointed out, the highest reality will come on terms that match your own situation, as the very ingredient that has been missing. In other words, you will experience God as that which makes you whole. If you're lonely, God comes as the feeling of divine companionship. If you're confused, God comes as insight and wisdom. If you feel limited and trapped by your inner and outer circumstances, the sacred presence will come as freedom. Or, if you have been in darkness, God will come as light.

Obviously, recognizing God is somewhat different for each person. The key is to know what to expect for yourself. Then, as you get more and more fully in harmony with your spiritual mission, you can expect to feel the presence of God in this way more often. It probably won't come every hour of every day. However, the gift of encounters with the sacred, coming as they do on personally meaningful terms, is a sign that you are on track with your soul's purpose.

4. *Recognizing purposefulness all around you.* Things in your life are happening for a purpose, but things are also occurring in the lives of other people around you for a purpose. Even if you think you've found your mission in life, don't become spiritually smug and think, "I've found my soul's purpose, and the heck with everyone else."

In fact, as you get more completely in touch with your own mission, it sensitizes you to perceive how all of life is purposeful. This is not to say everyone is aware of his or her soul's purpose and actively involved in its expression. Unfortunately, conditions in today's world are far from that. However, the Higher Self of each individual is continually active. It leads the conscious, personality self into situations and events that have the potential for spiritual awakening. Purposeful things are happening in everyone's life, despite the fact that most people are ignorant of what's going on.

If you're fulfilling your authentic mission, expect this by-product: perception of the reasons and meaning of the trials and the opportunities of those around you. When you notice this kind of sharpened awareness emerging within you, take it as a confirming sign. Then make constructive use of this sensitivity, not by preaching or offering unsolicited psychic readings, but through gentle, patient encouragement.

5. *Joy*. More than any other emotion, joy indicates that you're successfully on track with your destiny. More and more often you feel a delight from living. One Cayce reading even made this promise: Greater joy comes from expressing what you were truly born to do than could ever arise from doing things for power or fame. Admittedly, another person's mission may bring him or her great influence or notoriety, but it comes as an outgrowth and not as the goal itself.

In the past few months, how often have you felt joyous? If that emotion came to you more often, would you notice it? If so, then this quality is an especially good one to watch for as you act on your research game plan.

6. *Feeling energized*. As you live your spiritual mission, you begin to tap levels of energy that seem to come from beyond your personal resources. Often you will have the experience of getting "extra creative juices." You will develop greater stamina and persistence.

Of course, even the person fulfilling his or her mission still has days of being exhausted and tired. Life is demanding and some days simply take it out of you. Nevertheless, when you are in touch with something bigger than yourself, when your focus for living resonates with a larger plan, there are times when you seem to catch a second wind. An inner resource of strength and vitality becomes available. Those moments are a reminder you're in tune with the life direction your soul has chosen.

7. *A natural flow of events.* No doubt you've had the experience of being at the right place at the right time. It's amazing to discover that someone with just the skill you require comes into your life at the moment of greatest need. Or an opportunity may cross your path at just the time when you were looking for a new direction. These incidents seem to flow naturally without your having to make special efforts to plan or create them.

When something like this happens, you probably feel gratitude, but you may also wonder why you were so lucky. Maybe luck wasn't involved. Perhaps events that appear fortuitous suggest a deeper purpose. They can intimate that you are successfully applying the valid statement of your mission in life.

For this research project you are a spiritual investigator looking for confirmation of your soul's purpose. Keep an eye out for some or all of these seven signposts: a sense of wonder, seeing others benefit from your efforts, feeling the presence of God, recognizing purposefulness all around you, joy, feeling energized, and a natural flow of events. They may begin to occur more frequently as you apply the practical steps for testing your tentative mission statement.

If *none* of these signposts appear more often in your life, you probably should conclude that a new hypothesis is required for your research. It means going back to the exercises in chapter 4 and trying to formulate a revised wording for your mission.

However, this doesn't mean *all* of your small-step practical applications must be stunning achievements. You'll probably find that some tests fail. They look good on paper and even seem to be a natural fit with your mission statement, but when it comes to acting on them, the results are disappointing. Expect a few flops because no one is likely to come up with a foolproof game plan. And remember that if all your tests work out, you're probably not being adventuresome enough in experimenting with the limits and possibilities of your mission.

CHAPTER 6

Money and Resources for Living Your Purpose

MONEY. IS IT the key to happiness? Or is the love of money "the root of all evils," as the Bible suggests (1 Timothy 6:10)? No cliché can capture the truth of this important but complex issue in human affairs. It's an inescapable fact that you live in an economic world. No matter how spiritual you hope to be, you're sure to deal with financial realities whether you aspire to wealth or not.

Some people on a spiritual quest want to ignore vital economic matters. They overreact to mainstream society's preoccupation with money. They see the error in allowing the accumulation of money to become one's purpose in life. However, they fail to recognize how financial resources have a place in fulfilling their missions. The trick is to keep money in the role of a means to some higher aim, rather than let it become the goal itself.

Jacob Needleman's extraordinary book, *Money and the Meaning of Life*, addresses this intersection of finances and the quest for a higher purpose. Published in 1991, it's as timely and relevant as ever. Needleman's experience as a lifelong seeker of truth and decades as a university philosophy professor provide him with invaluable insights about integrating our lives—the mundane and the transcendent. One of his central points in the book is that we don't take money seriously enough. That idea sounds strange upon first hearing it because it would seem our culture is overly concerned with money matters. But maybe preoccupation is not the same thing as taking something seriously. He invites us to look more deeply at exactly what money represents and why it's crucial that we deal with these matters carefully and attentively. As Needleman describes it, taking money seriously means that "one gives to one's material needs the energy and intelligence that is required for satisfying them, while allowing space in oneself for the appearance and action of the striving for transcendent meaning."*

Money is about energy. As he puts it, "In our times, the forces that define human life on earth manifest themselves through money."† But it hasn't always been this way. In human history there have been many different ways of measuring or representing the life force and power—for example, ownership of land, or livestock, or human slaves, or water, or destructive weapons. For today's world it's especially money that serves as a measure of the movement of energy. And if we want to find and live a purposeful, meaningful life, then

---

* Jacob Needleman, *Money and the Meaning of Life* (New York: Doubleday, 1991), p. 51.
† Ibid, p. 40.

we must find ways to deal consciously and intentionally with the sphere of money.

Another central point to Needleman's important book concerns the question of where we actually *find* meaning. This inquiry is not so much about *what* the meaning of one's life entails, but instead *where* to even find it. He suggests that it is always to be found in the "intermediate"—in that place between the transcendent and the mundane, between the spiritual and the material. This idea is reminiscent of a principle from the Cayce readings: Only in the Christ-consciousness do extremes meet (1842-1). Similarly, for Needleman, it's this point of intersection between the higher and the lower where we can find and live a meaningful, purposeful life. "Human life has meaning only insofar as we consciously and intentionally occupy two worlds at the same time. One force alone can never bring meaning into human life. Meaning appears only in the place between the worlds, in the relationship of two worlds, two levels, two fundamental qualities of power and energy."* And because in today's world money is the primary representation of energy and force in the physical world, it's a factor we simply cannot ignore in our quest to live a soul purpose.

The Laws of Supply

As vital as it is to deal purposefully and intentionally with money, it's not the only form of "supply" in our lives. Let's

* Ibid, p. 43.

consider how we can broaden the exploration. Living your soul's purpose requires several different types of resources. In addition to financial assets, you may need an ample amount of time, food, energy, health, and friendship. They are the ingredients from material life that you'll use to accomplish your mission. Material resources are like different-colored paints on an artist's palette. He can blend them and innovate with them. In fact, the more colors, the more flexibility he has for creating something beautiful. Fortunately the dynamics that govern the flow of money also apply to any other form of material resource. There's only one set of rules you'll need to learn. To understand the role of money and other sources of supply, keep in mind this basic principle: Physical life obeys spiritual laws.

Some people disagree with this concept because they want to explain events in the simplest cause-and-effect way. The majority of the world's most respected economists would scoff at the notion that hidden forces help to shape financial conditions. They are unprepared to deal with the invisible side of reality. And yet, these highly educated leaders are at a loss to interpret many of the ups and downs of national and world economy. Is it because their statistical models haven't yet measured all the physical factors? Or do they need an expanded concept of economic life—one that appreciates intangible components such as consciousness, ideals, and values along with concrete ones such as money supply, interest rates, and debt load?

The philosophy found in the Cayce readings certainly offers a balanced view on these themes. In their readings many people asked questions about material resources. Money was the most frequent topic, but other types of supply were issues as well. Cayce's fundamental response was that each of us must first understand supply. How it operates in our lives will never make sense until we see exactly what it is.

We have many mistaken ideas about material resources, especially money. The erroneous concepts miss the mark, not because they are totally wrong, but because of the limited picture they portray. Too often our traditional image of money doesn't tell the whole story. For example, money isn't just a way of keeping score. In a sports-oriented culture it's easy to pick up this metaphor and try to overgeneralize its applicability. We're preoccupied with the question of who is winning and who is losing, so a competitive model makes us inclined to see amounts of money as points on a scoreboard. Nor is money most basically a method for keeping track of who has power over whom. Mainstream culture sees itself in hierarchical, pyramidal structures in which authority is exerted over subordinates. Since bosses have clout over employees, they should make more money, or so that line of thinking goes.

The problem with these explanations for money is they fail to include all the forces involved in the economic picture. Perhaps having a big bank account is somewhat like scoring lots of points. Maybe your boss should make a higher salary if her job requires more training or if she has to take on more responsibility than you. However, neither of those two models accounts for the element that Cayce put at the heart of his economic theory: "*sources* of supply are . . . *spiritual* in nature" (815-3).

It may be difficult to swallow the idea that material sup-ply, particularly money, is essentially a spiritual commodity. The church world has spent centuries teaching in direct and subtle ways that money is ungodly. Two favorite biblical ex-amples have often been cited: Jesus's statement to "Render therefore to Caesar the things that are Caesar's" (Matthew 22:21) and his warning "How hard it will be for those who have riches to enter the kingdom of God" (Mark 10:23).

It's debatable what Jesus may have truly meant by those comments, but the impact they've had on centuries of reli-gious life is quite clear. A strong tradition sees financial mat-ters as tainted and unholy. It implies that we deal with money only because it's unavoidable; we have to as physical crea-tures. Those who have that deeply entrenched mind-set have trouble imagining that the force of God is potentially alive and active in the medium we call money. However, that's exactly the point made by the Cayce readings: All life springs from the same divine source. Any form of supply in material life—including money, energy, and time—is the creative force of God. If money is associated with evil, it's only be-cause of the values and motives we attach to it. We can just as easily use loving ideals to create what we or others need out of financial resources.

The idea of abundance is one of the most useful ways to explore the spiritual underpinnings of material supply. The Cayce readings even refer to a law of abundance as one of the basic principles that govern our experiences. At first we may be inclined to think of laws as constraints, like traffic regulations or bureaucratic red tape. However, a more hopeful point of view recognizes that laws exist to help us. A universal law is a principle that describes how things operate everywhere and always. Whether we consciously understand the law or not, it influences our experiences. Universal laws are neutral, but we make use of them to our benefit or detriment.

Think of life as a game, one that has rules that direct the movements of its players. Any kind of game needs rules in order to be meaningful. Imagine trying to play softball, badminton, or poker without any guidelines. The action would be chaotic because you wouldn't know how to relate to the other players. The game would proceed haphazardly.

Laws exist in the game of life to serve the higher purpose of our own spiritual development. They can be called universal laws because they are applicable to everyone. Most universal laws are best understood in a format that states, "*If* you do something, *then* here are the results you can count on." For example, if you sow good seeds, then you will reap good fruit. Some of the universal rules pertain only to the physical level of existence. Mainstream science is continually providing a better understanding of those laws through research in fields such as physics, chemistry, geology, and biology.

Consider this simple example: The law of gravity is a rule in the game of life. If we drop a rock off a bridge, it will fall into the water below. The process is predictable and reliable. The law of gravity doesn't exist to restrict or trouble us. If we couldn't count on it, things might become a lot more difficult. In fact, certain things are possible only if we work consciously in cooperation with it. Imagine trying to stand up without gravity. Or think about how a skillful aeronautics engineer designs a jet aircraft to work in harmony with gravity and other laws to make flight possible. Even the beauty of a waterfall would be impossible without gravity as a rule of physical life.

Universal laws do not pertain just to physical life. In addition to material existence you have a mind and spirit. And so, not surprisingly, rules govern the invisible realm too. These universal laws describe the effects of attitudes, emotions, values, and ideals. Often what starts out in the hidden side of life later has an impact in the physical world.

Rules for the intangible world may sound esoteric and mysterious. And yet these rules for the game of life are "open secrets." Anyone who is willing to search with care and sincerity is sure to discover them. These universal laws are open to understanding because they are available through all the great spiritual teachers. In the words of the Christ and the Buddha, just to name two, we find a description of these principles, the law of abundance among them.

It's within our reach to comprehend how supply and abundance work. It's even a part of what we're supposed to learn from physical life. Spiritual growth happens as we work cooperatively with the law of abundance and use material resources to fulfill the purpose for which we were born. This sort of accomplishment is the birthright of everyone.

One person questioned Cayce on this very point. Living in the midst of the Great Depression, a forty-eight-year-old bookkeeper found herself in a desperate situation. She was head of a household, supporting her sister and son. Recently her married daughter and grandson had moved in too. In her reading she asked, "Is there a possibility that we may learn to use the law that Jesus used in controlling those things material and spiritual to meet present needs?" The answer could hardly have been more direct or encouraging: "This can be the experience of all" (303-6).

Actually, it can be misleading to speculate whether the law of abundance is yet functioning in your life. A universal law is always working in human experience. Rather, the question is whether you are consciously cooperating with the law to bring results that match your purpose in life. You can fight the law of abundance; you can thoughtlessly use it to create and maintain shortages in your life. For example, if you are fearful of shortages and therefore hoard money and other resources, then you can expect this universal law to fulfill your fears. On the other hand, you can just as readily operate in harmony with the law of abundance. The Cayce readings describe precisely how to do that.

Twelve Steps to Abundance and Prosperity

Something extraordinary emerges when we piece together Cayce's statements made to many different people on the subject of material resources: We discover a twelve-step program for working in conscious harmony with the law of supply and abundance.

If you follow these steps, *you can attract needed resources to*

start achieving the highest purpose of your life. This program is
no easy solution to the problem of shortage. It's not a shortcut, because there are none. Some of the stages will be especially demanding. They may ask you to let go of old beliefs or
familiar practices. Certain steps may require more patience
than you think you have, yet be persistent. The demands may
seem imposing, but the rewards probably can't come any
other way.

Think of this approach as a series of exercises through
which you will cycle many times in your life. It's not a method
you follow just once, like an inoculation that provides lifetime immunity. These steps need ongoing application in order to change your experience of material supply. In fact,
some of the steps may sound familiar because they reflect
principles with which you've already worked in previous
chapters of this book.

1. *Determine an overall purpose for your life; recognize your
mission.* This is a step you've already taken. You've formulated an educated best guess about your soul's purpose by writing a mission statement for testing. But
why is that step so important to the law of abundance?
Aren't there plenty of rich people who have no sense of
higher purpose, no personal mission that serves others
and leads to their own spiritual growth?

Society abounds with people who appear to be getting away with something when it comes to money matters. It can all seem so unfair. It's hard to reconcile belief

in a God of justice with the activities we see in the modern financial world. Yet somehow the laws are at work. Those with tremendous resources may have earned the opportunity to be responsible for so much material supply. This is the perspective of the Cayce readings, and they use the concept of reincarnation to help explain why the causes of great wealth aren't always visible.

However, reincarnation is not the answer to everything. Suppose a soul has wisely and constructively used material resources in a previous lifetime. The current incarnation might provide an opportunity to once again deal with affluence. But that's not an excuse to take advantage of others or to use prosperity as leverage against other people. Laws of karmic responsibility—that is, each of us will eventually reap what we have sown—are surely just as operative as the law of abundance.

A sense of mission is important because it defines a use for abundance. Consider this analogy: Tremendous rainfall can be a great blessing *if* there are riverbeds to direct its flow and irrigation ditches to distribute it to the crop fields for many days afterward. Without such channels to capture, store, and direct this abundance, all that rain can become a damaging flood. The same idea pertains to your life: You need to clearly define spiritual purposes to prepare you for prosperity. Until this first step has been taken, having too much too soon may create more obstacles than you can handle. Once you have a mission clearly in mind, abundance, which will come in many different forms, can be used for constructive, creative purposes.

2. *Identify shortages in your life.* Try to stand aside and objectively observe all the situations you currently face. Pay special attention to areas in which you're feeling frustration or disappointment. They are often spots where you can recognize shortages. Notice where you experience a lack of some sort. It could be a shortage of money, knowledge, health, friendship, free time, or any other resource for living.

Let's consider four hypothetical people for this and the next step. These examples are simple and may miss some of the complexities of life, but they portray themes you could encounter too. Each sample person confronts a difficulty that is linked to some kind of lack.

Eric is exasperated with a constant shortage of free time. His life seems to demand success in many more projects than he can ever complete. He divides his time into so many pieces that nothing is ever achieved with quality. And what's just as troublesome, no time is left over for relaxation.

Diane faces a different frustration. At the end of the month there are always more bills than there are available dollars. In her financial life she feels like she's always running to catch up with herself. She tries to follow a budget, but she continually meets a cash flow problem.

Anita experiences a shortage in her professional life. She would like to get into a different line of work but doesn't have the education required for a better position. Her biggest deficit is knowledge and job skills that could help her get ahead.

And finally, Alan is disappointed with a scarcity of emotional support as he wrestles with some painful challenges. He can't find anyone who will take time to listen to him. He knows he needs help to understand his confusion. For him the greatest shortage is friendship.

Spend some time observing your own life. The areas you identify in which you are lacking may resemble these examples or be quite different. Make note, either mentally or written, of the shortages you see.

3. *Recognize the purpose or lesson in each shortage.* Every kind of scarcity has the potential to be a spiritual lesson. When we experience a lack, there may be something to learn from it. Of course, it's a human tendency to want to avoid painful lessons. Or, when things do hurt, we usually desire the remedy as quickly as possible. When we have a lack of money, time, energy, or love, there is typically only one thing on our minds: Get the supply flowing, and fast.

However, avoidance of our lessons is not cooperation with the law of abundance. A painful or uncomfortable shortage is an announcement that something in us needs to be changed. It works the same way with the physical body. A painful condition such as a toothache or a swollen knee is a symptom. It's the body's way of calling attention to a deeper problem. Taking medication such as aspirin can mask the symptom, but it probably doesn't make the changes that are needed for real healing.

Painful shortages of money, time, energy, and love work the same way. Listen to the condition. Let it be your teacher. Ask yourself, "What is it showing me? What does it make me appreciate more deeply?"

Cayce gave this type of advice to many people, including a fifty-five-year-old woman who was barely making it financially. In fact, she didn't have the money to join Cayce's organization and obtain a reading, so special provisions were made. The reading was done immediately, and she was invited to make small installment payments whenever she could.

Her life reading identified her soul's purpose. Her calling was to help people better fit themselves into new life situations. This mission entailed assisting many different types of individuals to find fresh lifestyle patterns as they faced new locations, duties, obligations, or conditions. She was told about the sort of people she might especially be good at helping: expectant mothers, people setting up a new home, and those about to journey to foreign lands.

But this woman was troubled by several aspects of her life. She asked five questions at the end of her reading. First she wondered, "Is the work I'm doing what I came into this incarnation to do?" (1897-1). Cayce's answer was that she was very near to the aim. In many ways her occupation at the time—social welfare work—provided a setting with many occasions to serve in a way that would fulfill her mission. Other activities beyond her formal job also had a role to play, but many of her best opportunities were already at hand.

Second, she asked if she was studying with the correct spiritual teachers. The reading reminded her not to take what comes from others as law, but to apply and experience for herself the ideas she was learning.

The final three questions all dealt with issues of supply. She asked, "Why are my living quarters so humble and income so limited?" The answer may have surprised her. It began with the words: "That ye may better comprehend" (1897-1). In other words, there was something for her to understand about life that could come out of this shortage. The answer went on to affirm that conditions could improve, but the starting point was to learn from the situation.

Next she said, "Associates borrow from me but seldom return . . . Why is this?" (1897-1). She may not have wanted to hear the answer. It suggested that such behavior was a part of her own experience. She was warned that before each judgment in cases like this she would need to consider how she would be likely to act if the tables were turned.

Her final question dealt with another form of deficit: "Why are my friends so limited?" Cayce's brief response put the responsibility right back on her: "These are limited only because ye limit them" (1897-1). Her experience of supply was related directly to her own attitudes and actions.

Cayce was trying to direct this woman to the best way to respond to shortages, but a range of inner reactions is available. Let's consider some of the possibilities in the previous four hypothetical situations. Eric reacts to his lack of free time with self-criticism. It's admirable that he's able to take an objective look at his life and see how personal decisions have brought this situation on himself. However, he goes further, and by blaming himself creates a feeling of guilt.

Diane has a different reaction. She worries and pictures every conceivable catastrophe that may result from her dilemma of not having enough money. Many nights she can't get to sleep because of her imaginings.

Anita responds to her shortage of knowledge by blaming others. She's quick to recall that grade school teachers caused her to hate formal education. She remembers that her parents forced her to enter the job market upon graduation from high school. They gave no serious consideration to college for her. Anita is very good at attributing her problems to other people.

Alan has a more constructive reaction. He's able to respond to his shortage of emotional support with patience and self-reflection. He sees clearly how much he wants and needs friends; however, he also recognizes a lesson in his situation. It's not hard for him to recall circumstances in which he wasn't a very supportive friend to someone else in need. His lack of friends now is teaching him just how important friendship is. It's a

mature attitude that doesn't let him feel sorry for himself or deny the authentic lack that he faces.

4. *Use what you have at hand.* Make the best possible use
of what you already have. Additional resources come as
you are a good steward of what is at hand. This principle
is common sense. It probably governs the way you give
to others. For example, suppose you are considering a
contribution to a certain charitable organization. First
you look into its purpose and its current operation. If
you discover that the organization wastes money and
mistreats employees, you probably aren't going to add
to its resources with any of your money. Or suppose you
volunteer to tutor a high school student who is having
trouble in mathematics. If you later find this student is
not really trying hard and is wasting your efforts, how
likely are you to keep giving your knowledge and time?
You might give that student the benefit of the doubt for
a while, but a time will likely come when it's in no one's
best interest for things to continue that way.

What does it mean for you to be a good steward of
your own resources? The process is important, whether
you are responsible for great amounts or small. It's the
little things that count in life. Something remarkable
happens whenever you take the best possible care of even
your most inconsequential possessions: You put yourself
in harmony with the law of supply and abundance—you
show that you can be trusted with more.

It all begins with your basic attitudes toward your

resources: your money, home, and possessions. In the deepest sense they aren't yours. They are available to you, on loan from the universal source of supply. As one Cayce reading puts it, "That which is in the material world is as lent us of the Lord" (2667-6). Take care of things the way you would if you knew they had to be returned to their true owner.

The same attitude goes for your talents and abilities. In Cayce's long-range view of soul development and reincarnation, he suggests that abilities not used for constructive purposes are then lost. Remember the parable of the talents (Matthew 25:14–30). In this case, talents are a denomination of money used in Roman times. Before departing on a journey, a wealthy man entrusted portions of his money to three stewards. While he was away, two of the three put the money to work and through wise investing increased the sum for their master. However, the third steward was fearful and buried the money because he wanted to be sure that none would be lost. Upon his return the wealthy master was furious at the one who had failed to make use of what he had been given. Jesus's message is not necessarily an endorsement of free enterprise or capitalism, but rather a reminder that our resources are meant to be put to use.

Proper timing is a second way to make good use of what is at hand. The phrase "flow of supply" implies movement. Try to respond in a timely fashion with your supply whenever it is available. Although this principle is most clearly demonstrated with money, you can probably find other resources to which it also applies. At its best, this idea means responding immediately instead of delaying, procrastinating, and indirectly hoarding what you have. If someone else's experience of supply depends directly on your payment of a bill, keep the flow going in as timely a manner as you can. That's part of being a good steward.

A third method involves investing in your ideals. To what extent does the way you spend your money, time, and energy reflect your own values? You can follow simple procedures to work with this concept or you can make it quite elaborate; the choice is yours. However, the fact is that you support and in a sense vote for certain things in the world around you by the way you spend your money, time, and energy. A part of making the best use of what you already have is to do this consciously, so as to support your values and ideals. Here are two examples.

One man is particularly conscious of how his own values are expressed by little decisions he makes in everyday life. His ideals in life are hope, positive affirmation, and peace. Therefore, he's made two commitments concerning how he spends his time and his dollars. First, he's very careful about the television programs to which he gives his time and attention. Most of what's available doesn't match his personal ideals. And so, although it severely limits his options, he watches only those television shows that have a positive message. Second, he's very aware of the implicit values contained in children's toys. Many are based on war and aggression, and he refuses to buy them for his children. Both of these commitments reflect his own best values.

Another person makes a different sort of resolution. She's fortunate enough to usually have a little extra money to invest at the end of each month. What does she do with these discretionary funds? She wants her investments to reflect her ideals of love and world peace. She's willing to take the additional time required to research companies to make sure her investments reflect those ideals. She continues to purchase stock in corporations whose products and practices she can believe in. Occasionally she ends up getting a somewhat smaller yield on her money than she might otherwise. However, it's worth it to her because she knows she's working cooperatively with the law of abundance.

There is a basis directly from the Cayce readings for what is now called "socially sensitive" investing. The best illustration is from a business reading given to a forty-seven-year-old sales executive. He posed the simple question "Are my investments properly made?" The answer from Cayce recommended broadening the criteria upon which financial decisions were to be conducted. "If [the investments] are for increase only, without honest service given, you'd better change them. If they are those that God Himself may smile upon, invest all the more!" (2409-1).

The follow-up question from this businessman was just as significant: "Is my desire to accumulate wealth in order to render service to humanity a laudable one?"

Cayce the spiritual psychologist was at his best with the answer. He told the man that the aim was admirable, but to be careful. He shouldn't wait until he became rich before starting to serve humanity; service should begin even while finances were still scarce. The final words of Cayce's response pointed to how easily the best of intentions can get sidetracked, particularly when it comes to money. "For, if one cannot render service though his income will barely keep body and soul together, even if it were tripled or multiplied by a million he would not do any better!" (2409-1).

Years earlier another person had been given a similar message when he asked about using the profits from commercial enterprises to help the work of Edgar Cayce. He was cautioned about making great plans if he wasn't already doing all he could to be of assistance. "He that will not use that already in hand would not use same were it a hundredfold more. . . . Use that in hand and the increase comes with the use" (5502-4).

5. *Dispel fear, doubt, and anxiety.* These emotions prevent the law of supply and abundance from making your life more prosperous. Where do fears, doubts, and anxieties most frequently come up? For many people it's about financial security, but these troublesome emotions can attach themselves to any aspect of supply for living.

A major contributor to this problem may be negative statements repeated silently as a form of inner talk. Do you ever catch yourself feeding words like these to your emotional nature?

- There's not going to be enough.
- I'll never be able to get it all done.
- Where are other people when I need them?
- I'll never learn how to do this.

Each one of these negative thoughts reflects fear, doubt, or anxiety about the future. Each example denies abundance and supply. One is fear that there won't be enough time. Another is doubt about sufficient personal energy. A third is there won't be adequate support from other people. And the final example is anxiety that there won't be the knowledge that is needed.

When you recognize one of your own limiting mind-sets, what can you do to dispel the paralyzing effect? The most potent method is to see clearly how fears, doubts, and anxieties are self-fulfilling. Anxiety that you will be short of money tends to create that very condition. Fear that there may not be enough time makes you rush and use time inefficiently, fulfilling the fear. Doubts about levels of personal energy actually drain you of energy. Desperately worrying about receiving loving support from others tends to make you not very lovable. Fears about insufficient knowledge can block your capacity to learn. Merely understanding these facts may give you the motivation to make some changes.

Usually the best way to get rid of a troublesome attitude or emotion is replacement rather than repression. What outlook on life is the finest substitute for fear, doubt, or anxiety? The answer is the next step in this twelve-part approach.

6. *Maintain a thankful attitude.* Genuine appreciation is a powerful tool to put you in harmony with the law of abundance. You probably have a lot for which to be thankful. Virtually everyone does. No doubt some people suffer greatly, but even they are often able to muster the capacity to see things for which they are truly thankful.

   Too easily we can get caught up in the busyness of living and forget to be grateful. Feeling thankful is not a denial of life's realities. It's not a retreat into a Polly-anna worldview that sees only sweetness and light. Rather, deeply felt appreciation is an affirmation of the goodness of life. It's a refusal to let the inevitable chal-lenges of life obscure one's sight of blessings and won-derful moments.

7. *Give a regular percentage of your resources (monetary and otherwise).* Sharing your resources is a key to the law of abundance. Giving makes room for more to come into your life. Of course, the principle works not only for money, but for any form of supply. And you may dis-cover a crossover effect. When you give in one way, resources flow back into your life in another form. Giving generously of your free time may result in friendship or creative energy coming back to you. Do-nating money sets in motion a process that may bring greater knowledge or fresh ideas into your life.

   You might find it's helpful to make certain commit-ments about the amount and frequency of giving. For

example, set a particular percentage of income to donate or a specific number of hours per week to volunteer. The guidelines don't have to be rigid, but they
describe a direction and goal you are shooting for.
Without a clear plan in mind, it's easy to get distracted
and forget to maintain patterns of giving.

8. *Remove any competitive attitude. Help others toward success.* The Cayce readings present another version of the
law of abundance: If you fulfill the law of supply and
abundance in the experience of someone else, then
what you need will abundantly come to you. In other
words, positive human relations can play a big role in
how you experience the law of abundance.

This version of the law of abundance was presented to
an unemployed forty-four-year-old man. In his life reading he was told explicitly the nature of his mission: to
work to unite the efforts of many. Cayce even suggested
one expression of this mission in which he was likely to
succeed. The reading (1946-1) encouraged the man to
get involved in assisting farmers to unite their efforts. It
concluded with the promise that he would discover his
own prosperity by helping other people to find theirs.

Focusing exclusively on your own prosperity can
even be counterproductive. Economic life is a social
phenomenon, something done in relationship to others.
There is no genuine prosperity accomplished as a private
affair. Sometimes what may appear to be wealth—viewed
solely in terms of dollars accumulated—is achieved at
the expense of others. But true abundance, a flow of

supply that brings joy, comes in community with other people. As you help friends and associates experience the positive aspect of the law of abundance, it brings the same thing into your life.

9. *Hold an attitude of positive expectancy.* Feel with your whole self that the law of abundance is reliable. Expect that you will receive exactly what you need in order to take the next steps toward your soul's purpose. Expect a miracle. Anticipate that as you give out, resources will flow back to you.

However, be sure to keep an open mind along with your positive expectations. You may not know in advance how abundance will come into your life; its appearance or type of expression can vary. You might give of your time and knowledge and find that it flows back to you in the form of love or health. You might give of your money or energy and find that it returns as joy or peace of mind. All supply is based on one fundamental source: the spiritual life force.

Remember that the universe is creatively playful with you. It attracts to your life just what you need most. You can expect to observe this process, and you can rely on it.

The Cayce readings add another point to the subject of expectancy: the distinction between contentment and satisfaction. Although these words are often used synonymously, they have subtly different connotations. A person who is satisfied neither wants nor expects anything more. Someone else who is content may recognize continuing needs and expect their fulfillment, but that individual patiently awaits the right timing.

Cayce emphasized this contrast in a reading given for a thirty-seven-year-old woman. In many ways her situation was like that of hundreds of others who received life readings. In her request to Cayce for help, she spelled out her strong desire to get a clearer sense of meaning and purpose. She wrote in April 1926:

My dear Mr. Cayce,

Will you give me one of your Life Readings? I am particularly interested to find out the reason for the Saturn-like restrictions placed on my life, subtle holdings back which keep me from fully expressing and doing. . . . I feel there is *something* for me to *do* but cannot find that something. . . . I want to speedily set my feet upon the path of my true endeavor. To find myself in the larger sense.

Very truly yours,

Her reading offered specific guidance about her mission. She was told that her calling was "to teach in the way of service to the young, and especially to those of the adolescent period" (2842-1).

She found this first reading helpful but felt stuck in her old ways of life. She asked for further assistance and for her second reading posed this financial problem: "Have I a right to demand abundance, or should I be content with my small income?" Cayce's higher source first responded, "Be *content* with what thou hast, but never be *satisfied* with what thou hast." In other words, she needed to start with peace of mind and patience about her situation, but not feel blocked permanently. Then it went on to tell her the key to contentment: Reflect the creative energy (that is, give out to the world) and then expect an abundance will come back. "Put thine self in that attitude, that position, of reflecting that as is of the Creative Energy, and that necessary—and over an abundance—will be in thine hand" (2842-2).

10. *Affirm that you will have what you need to grow spiritually and fulfill your mission.* An important distinction must be made at this step. What is a *need* and what is a *want*? For example, remember the head of a financially troubled household who asked Cayce about mastering the law of supply and abundance in order to "meet present needs" (303-6). Even though the answer given in the reading was encouraging, there was a catch. Exactly what were the authentic needs of her family?

The law of abundance can provide all that you need to fulfill your mission in life. That may not be the same thing as all you want. Some desires come from your personality self rather than your individuality. For example, another recipient of a Cayce reading was having a rough time with material necessities and wondered if this was because she had not sufficiently sought the kingdom of God first. She remembered the biblical promise that "all these things shall be yours as well" (Matthew 6:33), and she worried that she hadn't done her part adequately to seek God first.

Cayce's answer probably fit both her condition and our own. Initially he stated that a more diligent, sincere search for God was necessary. Then he added, "Most of us think we need a great deal more than we do!" (2628-9). What a reminder! *We have to evaluate our standard of evaluation.* We need to measure honestly what our real needs are. Maybe the law of abundance is already operating in our lives more than we realize. Perhaps the great majority of resources required to fulfill our missions are currently at hand. In an age of consumerism and commercial bombardment, it's not easy to sort out authentic needs from manufactured wants.

11. *Trust that God gives the increase.* You will reach a point with each shortage situation where you know you have done all you can do. With optimism and enthusiasm, simply trust. You've done your part; now let God add to what you've done and manifest an abundance for you.

Trust also that the timing will be right. You may have your own timetable in mind, but the law of abundance and supply works with its own rules for best timing. Exactly the things you need will come to you at just the proper moment.

This is one of the simplest of the twelve steps, yet for many people it's one of the most difficult. Sometimes we're like the worrisome baker who has put a pie in the oven but has to check on it every two minutes. We may find it hard to release our concerns, to remember that things are happening behind the scenes, and to affirm all that's needed now is our belief and trust.

12. *Receive the good that comes to you.* Maybe this step is obvious and doesn't need to be listed. However, some people get stuck right after step 11. As abundance begins to flow into their lives they find it hard to accept. They wonder whether they can really claim and embrace what is offered. Perhaps they don't feel worthy or they worry that somehow strings are attached.

Be assured that the good that flows into your life is meant for you. The only strings attached are responsibilities that come with the resources. Use them creatively and constructively to fulfill your spiritual purpose.

How Much Should I Give?

Giving is a paradox. In order to have abundance, you must be willing to give. To the analytical mind that doesn't make much sense. Logic argues that to have a lot of anything, you've got to save up whenever possible. For example, this line of thinking says that to be rich you must hang on to the money you have; to have plenty of energy or free time, you must jealously conserve what's available to you.

However, the Cayce readings on abundance and prosperity point in a different direction. For example: "Only that thou hast given away is thine" (585-4). Strange as it may sound, we never really own something unless we break our attachment to it. Giving away sometimes means literally turning over possession to someone else. But even more often it means releasing your tight grip and being willing to share.

It's a matter of attitude. Is money, time, energy, talent, or knowledge yours or is it God's? When you give it away, you don't squander the resource, but you use it wisely to benefit self and others. You keep sources of supply flowing by making sure they are used responsibly. This willingness to apply and to share what you have can then bestow an authentic kind of ownership, one that is invisible but lasting.

Most people take time to think about these issues only in special circumstances. They are challenged only when there is not enough or when there is too much. It's obvious shortage is a difficulty, but who would think of abundance as a problem? Yet it creates its own kind of dilemma: What will we do with the excess? In a sense, we define our relationship to the law of supply and abundance by the way we act in the face of abundant conditions.

What happens when you have extra money, a surplus of energy, or time on your hands? The question might make you smile to yourself and say, "I wish I had that problem more often." And yet, even if you face this happy prospect only infrequently, your behavior in these situations has a potent influence. Do you splurge the money, waste the energy, or kill the time? It might not seem so bad at the moment, but you've made a powerful statement about your attitude toward supply. You are creating conditions that can make abundance more difficult in the future.

For example, imagine a man with four children who has financial worries. His family doesn't live extravagantly, but money always seems to be tight. His wife has a part-time job as a substitute teacher, and he works as a carpenter. Sometimes there's plenty of work, but occasionally there are slack periods in which he has time on his hands. Suppose this man wastes that time. The periods of abundant free time don't get invested in any creative efforts that might help the family financially or otherwise. The time slips away as he oversleeps or watches television. This hypothetical person operates against the law of abundance.

What does it mean to work in harmony with the universal law? Follow the twelve steps already described in this chapter, from recognizing your mission in life to accepting the good that comes to you. But how does it all work? What hidden mechanism turns giving into receiving? Is it magic, or is it lawful principles?

The answer is rather simple. No magic is involved, but instead a rule of spiritual life: You attract your experiences by the way you define yourself. In other words, if your consciousness and your actions say loudly and clearly, "I'm blessed with resources," then life is likely to bring experiences that reinforce that self-image. On the other hand, if your attitudes and behaviors state, "I'm short on the things I want," then you merely attract greater shortage.

How can you act to define yourself as prosperous and

blessed? By giving to those who have greater needs than you. It works with money and any other kind of resource. When you think about people who have more than you and you desire to reach their level by hoarding what you've got, the results won't be what you hoped for. By defining yourself as poor—relative to those you aspire to match—you attract experiences to enhance your poverty. In contrast, what happens when you periodically remember those whose need is greater than your own and reach out to share with them? In those moments you define yourself as prosperous, relatively speaking. Consequently life will bring you situations to enhance that self-definition; abundance will flow into your life. No sorcery is involved. You create your circumstances by the way you define yourself in the world.

This rule may convince you that giving is important. However, many different styles and approaches of sharing are possible. One is to wait until you have something extra before you start giving. The problem with this philosophy is demand usually expands to meet available resources. The tendency is never to get around to sharing.

One case from the readings illustrates this point. A thirty-year-old man working in his family's jewelry business wrote to Cayce in the spring of 1930, "I am preparing to leave my present occupation. I am uncertain of my future as I have not yet found my real life work, and trust it will be more satisfactory and profitable. Could you help me in my problem with a Life Reading?" (520-1). The reading for this man identified many patterns in his life, one of which was his mission: to change the thoughts of people, especially through writing. But obviously success along a new life path was going to take some material resources.

One of the questions submitted by the man concerned wealth. He asked, "How much money must [I] accumulate to enable [me] to comfortably provide for [my] family?" The response was a statement about the inner dynamics of prosperity, particularly related to the act of giving: "Use that thou hast in hand! and he that will not contribute to the humanitarian interest with one *penny* above that needed from day to day, will *not* contribute were there *millions* at hand! *This* [is] a truth" (520-1). In other words, the waiting approach to giving doesn't work. We're just kidding ourselves if we try to adopt that style.

A second method is to give a precise amount of money, time, or energy on an unfailing schedule. Often this means to follow the biblical suggestion to tithe. This approach is fine if it's done with the right spirit. However, some people slip into thinking of it as an investment, just like their stock purchases or payroll savings deductions.

Imagine the hypothetical case of a businesswoman who is regular and exact with her monetary contributions. Each month she donates a strict ten percent of her paycheck. She read about prosperity consciousness and was open to this idea for achieving wealth. Unfortunately the article that introduced her to the concept of tithing presented the story in a self-centered way. Now she thinks that prosperity means just one thing: more money. Her tithe is like any other financial investment, except that she believes this one has a guaranteed profit. She's proud of herself for having figured out how God runs the universe, and she's ready to take advantage of that insight. She diligently makes sure that the exact 10 percent gets doled out. In fact, as far as she's concerned, it's unimportant to whom or to what she gives each month.

This woman is operating with half an understanding of the law of abundance. A commitment to giving is valuable, but the 10 percent figure may not be as magical as some people contend. What's the half of the picture she is missing? Abundance is a spiritual law. Whenever we work with this rule, the key is always *the spirit in which we do something*—our purpose and ideal. More important than the exact percentage is the proper spirit about what we are doing. God cannot be manipulated with clever tricks or sleight of hand maneuvers with our paychecks. Motives tell the story. In fact, we could say that this woman never really gives because strings are attached to her apparent gifts—expectations of reward that are selfish. Although dollars may change hands, at a deeper, spiritual level she has not fully surrendered the money because her motivation is to get more dollars back.

The third option is the best. It combines dedication with flexibility and concern. Flexibility allows room for growth. When you begin a giving program you may decide that 2 percent of your net income is all you can manage and still keep a good spirit about the process. Over time you may gradually increase the amount, but no single figure demands your rigid compliance.

Concern means that your contributions are carefully considered. You don't give simply to be giving. Each donation is thought out and seen as a way of supporting your values in the world. Every gift is a responsible act of stewardship with your resources. You might even ask prayerfully before each decision, "Where does God's work most need this money to go?"

When it comes to money, decide for yourself what percentage you can currently give. Make sure it's an amount you can donate with a loving, joyous spirit. Then make a commitment to that level and do it consistently. The regularity is crucial. You may be tempted to stop making contributions temporarily if times get tough and finances are tight. It's easy to make giving the first thing you strike from your budget when funds are short. Unfortunately, to do so is likely to produce the opposite effect of what you want. Maybe you'll need to readjust the percentage from time to time, but keep on giving at some level. To stop is to reinforce the notion of shortage and lack. Cutting off the outward flow can strengthen poverty consciousness and make it more difficult for needed resources to flow in to you. When times are tight is when you need to make sure you maintain some kind of giving with a joyful, thankful spirit.

Of course, giving means more than just financial contributions to needy people and charitable organizations. You can give also of your time, energy, talents, creativity, knowledge, and prayers. If you aren't yet ready to start a financial giving program, begin with some other form of supply. Gifts of time, knowledge, or loving support can be just as important for living in harmony with the law of abundance. Maybe later you'll feel ready to include money as well.

Finally, you should consider another way of giving: to yourself. This may sound strange, but properly understood it's an authentic need. Remember that your mission in life is meant to be lived in service to others *and* in relationship to yourself. Your soul's purpose includes the investment of time, talents, and energy so that your individuality self can grow. The same principle holds true for the way you use your money. Here are just a few ways that you might occasionally present yourself with a gift: Buy a book that's likely to help your personal growth. Get a massage. Take a couple of vacation hours to get off work early and spend time in nature. Buy more nutritious, whole food, even if it costs a little more.

Material resources have an important role to play in the fulfillment of your mission. Since your soul's purpose includes some kind of creative, practical involvement in the world, questions of physical supply are unavoidable. In fact, the material ingredients of life are simply spiritual forces at work. By themselves they are neutral, and it's up to you to infuse them with your values and ideals. God is the source of all supply, but you are a distributor of it.

Understanding how the law of supply and abundance operates is a tricky business. There's plenty of room for self-delusion and rationalization. It's easy for commonplace greed to masquerade as prosperity consciousness. Pride can enter the picture. Or, we may fall into the belief that some secret code of spiritual law has been deciphered and now we can manipulate God. This erroneous thinking assumes that God will be obliged to provide riches if we pay our 10 percent "dues" every month.

And yet, despite all the detours and dead ends that can distract us, understanding of and cooperation with the law of abundance are possible. As we joyfully share what we have, the very resources come to us that are most needed to fulfill our missions in life.

CHAPTER 7

Long-term Thinking: Jobs, Avocations, and Callings

THIS CHAPTER IS for anyone who wants to or must work for pay. It examines the question of how your job can fit your mission statement. If you are just about to enter the market-place, you'll find useful exercises in this section. If you are already employed but wondering if you can really fulfill your soul's purpose in that situation, this chapter will help you consider whether a change is appropriate. For some people this portion of the book is optional reading because they are retired, work at home caring for children or elderly parents, or for other reasons don't plan to be drawing a paycheck any-time soon.

Of course, your circumstances in life may be such that you perform the mission for which you were born outside of a formal occupation. Your success may come through volunteer work, hobbies, and interests. However, if economic condi-tions require that you make money from a job, then you probably would like to get double duty from that employment: earning an income so you can pay your bills *and* doing those things that fulfill a deeper calling.

It may not be easy to step into a job that gives you a spiritual sense of satisfaction. Many business environments are stressful and highly competitive. Bosses feel the pressure to produce material results and usually pass the tension on to their employees. However, you may well be able to find a niche that fits you, even if you have to create one for yourself.

No doubt many people are unhappy with their work situations. They feel frustrated, unappreciated, and caught in routines that don't make use of their best talents. On a regular basis most individuals in our society either change jobs or at least consider it seriously. This suggests that deep feelings of unfulfillment abound in the workplace. And there is survey research evidence to suggest that a very high percentage of workers feel disengaged from their jobs.

How can you avoid this sort of frustration? The problem shouldn't be due to a lack of job possibilities. Thirteen thousand different job titles were published by the U.S. Government Printing Office (GPO; now the Government Publishing Office) in the *Dictionary of Occupational Titles*. The GPO ceased publication of this dictionary in 1999 and replaced it with a much more flexible and accessible online database, the Occupational Information Network (O*NET), available at https://www.onetonline.org/. You may qualify for and be interested in only a tiny portion of the prospects you find, but even then, many options may be available to you.

Why might you contemplate changing employers or the

kind of work you do? Two reasons are most common. The first is that your current job really is out of sync with your mission in life. In such a situation it is useful to make a distinction. Does your work require actions that violate your ideals and values? Does it feel like you are actually going counter to your spiritual destiny? Or does your work feel more or less neutral—violating no personal ideals, but at the same time leaving you with wheels spinning and no sense of progress toward your mission? If you can clearly see that your present employment is actively taking you away from your soul's purpose, a change is called for as soon as possible. On the other hand, if you see that your job is neutral, you may want to explore some adjustments before moving on.

The second reason many people change employers is to get away from an uncomfortable setting. In some cases leaving is the only thing you can do. However, in other situations quitting is merely a method for evading some aspect of yourself that needs to be examined. Remember from chapter 2 the metaphor of a wheel. What happens if you are on the rim of the wheel as it turns? You feel as if you are moving in a new direction, only to discover that eventually you come back to the same point where you began. This can happen if you hop from job to job. When you make no changes in yourself, there is a strong likelihood you'll end up in similar circumstances with new people. This is not to say you must forever stay put, no matter how obnoxious you find your boss or fellow employees. However, honest self-appraisal should accompany any career change. Ask yourself, "What traits in myself have contributed to this problem? How can I change so that I don't repeat this experience with a new employer?"

The Case Against Changing Jobs

Several ideas from the Cayce readings emphasize the importance of dealing properly with your current job, even if you find it limiting or unfulfilling. The first priority is the responsibility you may have toward your family members. Repeatedly the Cayce readings insist that spiritual disciplines should make us better spouses, better parents, and better citizens. This principle speaks directly to anyone who imagines that his or her soul's purpose requires a drastic change at the expense of family members. If your family is economically dependent on you, a part of your soul's purpose involves meeting those responsibilities as best you can. It may require a delay in making the sort of job switch you'd prefer. It may necessitate patience on your part, but keep in mind that God is not anxious that you meet a particular timetable. You can be on track with your mission even when you are meeting obligations to loved ones and temporarily delaying a different line of employment.

The case against changing jobs includes a second kind of responsibility: to your fellow workers. Can your departure be a graceful one that demonstrates genuine concern for work colleagues and their needs? Can you leave without putting any more stress than necessary on your coworkers? Optimally your departure would be a win-win situation, in which everyone could benefit: You would profit by moving on to the next step in your destiny, and your fellow workers would profit from having known you and now having new opportunities.

Of course, the optimum isn't always easy to achieve. Conditions at work may have deteriorated to the point that your departure is sure to be difficult and tense. Even in this case, you can try to keep an inner, spiritual discipline as you move through the steps of leaving. Remember that your coworkers are souls, just like you. They are also trying to find their missions in life, even though it may not be a conscious search. Try to be patient and understand that some of their behaviors may grow out of a hidden sense of frustration or unfulfillment with their own work situations.

Another kind of problem can also make a job transition difficult. Coworkers with whom you have a good relationship may subtly try to make you feel guilty for leaving. They may present countless reasons why you must stay. They may see your departure as abandonment and imagine you're acting irresponsibly. How can you meet this attitude in coworkers in a loving way? How can you maintain both concern for them and commitment to what you know you need to do next in your life?

First, make sure you have given all you can to those who are likely to step in and take your place. This means sharing your knowledge, but even more important, supporting and encouraging those who will have new opportunities after you leave. Second, if it's possible, adopt a timetable for the transition that fits their needs just as much as it does your own. If you have some flexibility about when you will accept a new position, spend the time it will take to make your exit a graceful one. And finally, don't succumb to guilt. When a new job is authentically part of your soul's purpose, it doesn't hinder others. Some of your coworkers may not be able to see this fact at first, but their lack of self-confidence shouldn't hold you back.

Another idea from the Cayce readings suggests caution when it comes to changing jobs. The principle is to do everything you can with the situation at hand before discarding it for another one. Before you give up on your current place of employment, try all possibilities for securing a job that will give you chances to get in sync with your mission. Is it feasible to arrange some new job duties, even if you must retain many of the old ones? Your boss may be open to creating some new slants to your regular tasks, approaches that are more in line with your sense of life purpose. Sometimes just a few minor changes can make a big difference—even those that involve a short amount of time each day on a new activity.

If you find that your present position is a dead end, check on the chances of a transfer. Is another slot within the company conceivable? Search out all the options before concluding that you must work elsewhere.

A final word of caution about changing jobs concerns employment in general. When it comes to living your spiritual mission, no job may ever be totally "it." No work situation is likely ever to be the fulfillment of your soul's purpose all by itself. The mission statement is too broad to be limited in that way. Therefore you will need to look for ways to express your mission in addition to the way you earn money.

Volunteerism is a lifestyle pattern that makes room for service activities that are done simply out of love. The motivation is compassion for others—whether it's disabled children, senior citizens, or wildlife. It's also out of genuine love for oneself, a love that finds ways to use talents and abilities whether monetary reimbursement is involved or not.

Before you rush into a career change, you may want to consider joining the ranks of volunteerism. Try using some of your key talents outside of the ways you earn a living. Time may be restricted for you, and perhaps only an hour or two a week can be invested this way. But you may find that something alters when you regularly engage in free-time activities that are in accord with your mission statement. You may discover that you more easily accept your current work situation and are willing to strive patiently toward some long-term career changes.

How to Find the Right Job

In spite of the case against changing jobs now, you may find that this is the time in your life when a new form of employment is right. How can you make this adventure as painless and as fun as possible? A good place to start is identifying your options.

If you are already in the marketplace, you'll need to decide eventually whether you want to change careers or simply look for a new employer in the same line of work. If you want a new career, then you face many more choices, such as:

- Do I want one full-time job or a composite job
  in which I piece together several part-time
  positions?
- Do I want to work for an organization or be
  self-employed?
- Do I need to go back to school for further training?
  Am I willing and able to do so?

Of course, you're a step ahead of most people because
you've formulated a tentative wording for your mission statement. The questions you face are still tough ones, but you're
equipped with a sense of life direction that can help you evaluate the suitability of different options. At a deep level that
mission statement tells you what you want from life. It may
not directly answer the surface questions of exactly how you
will accomplish it, but it provides a profound solution into
which all the more practical answers will eventually fit.

It's like trying to put together a nine-piece jigsaw puzzle
that you've been told has one central piece and the other eight
arranged around it. Some people would try to solve the puzzle by fitting together first the outer pieces and then leaving
the last piece for its obvious placement in the middle. However, that's the hard approach. Since all eight outer pieces
interlock with the centerpiece, why not get it into position
initially? That's precisely what you've done by determining a
thematic statement of your soul's purpose. There may be
many outer expressions of that mission, but they all need to
interlock with that central answer you've chosen. Although
you may still face many questions about choosing the best

form of employment, you've got the advantage of a central answer that will hold everything together.

As you start your job search, remember the importance of your attitude. Nothing limits you faster than negative thoughts. Watch your inner talk and observe any statements you repeatedly make to yourself. Do any of them anticipate failure because of your handicaps? Perhaps you'll observe yourself silently saying words like these:

- I'm too inexperienced.
- I'm too young [or too old].
- I'm a woman and women never seem to get this sort of job.
- I'm from a racial minority.
- I haven't had a good enough education.

The potential list of limiting statements is much more extensive, but from these examples you can imagine what happens. Like a hypnotic suggestion, these words begin to shape the way you see yourself and the job world. To combat this tendency, just remember that we are all handicapped, some more obviously than others. Some impairments are the result of our own life conditions: physical disabilities, age, lack of education, or previous work experience. Other conditions are due to the shortcomings of the society in which we live: racial prejudice, gender discrimination, and so on. Some people's handicaps just show up a little more clearly than do those of others. Keep in mind that we all have limitations with which to deal.

Next, remember that thoughts you dwell on can be self-fulfilling. The more you let the limiting words control your self-concept and your thinking, the more likely it is that you won't land the job you want. Replace the restricting statements with positive, hopeful affirmations. People with limitations just like yours have made it in the past. You may have to work a little harder to get what you want because of some constraint, but make up your mind to do whatever it takes.

With the proper attitude—one that doesn't deny limitations but is willing to overcome them—you're ready to formulate a plan for finding the right job. Basically that plan is a strategy for matching your talents, mission statement, and temperament to the employment world. You already have two of the three ingredients: a list of your talents and a wording for your mission. The third factor, temperament, needs some explanation.

What is temperament? Seen from the distinction between personality and individuality, it's more closely related to the essential qualities of your individuality self. Temperament shapes the way you perceive, evaluate, and respond to life. It's more fundamental than any single talent. For example, two people could both have a gift for managing business affairs, but if their temperaments were different, the organizations they run would be dissimilar.

Many schemes and models for describing temperament have been proposed. The earliest may have been the four Greek humors: blood (sanguine temperament), black bile (melancholic), yellow bile (choleric), and phlegm (phlegmatic).

In more recent times Carl Jung suggested a model made up of several polarities. The first shows how each of us judges and evaluates life using either thinking or feeling functions. At no moment are we likely to do both simultaneously, and each person is temperamentally inclined to favor one side of the polarity over the other.

Another polarity concerns the way we perceive life: in terms of its here-and-now concreteness or its possibilities that have yet to materialize. Jung described this as a choice between two perceptual functions, sensation and intuition. Again, one's temperament predisposes him or her to favor one form of perception over the other.

In addition, Jung defined two basic attitudes toward life. One looks outward and focuses primarily on events in the surrounding world. He labeled this attitude extroversion, suggesting that it deals with inner matters only in the context of outer ones. Its mirror opposite is introversion—not so much shyness, but rather an attitude that focuses on inner life over outer. In the Jungian model each of us has a temperament that can be labeled in terms of our tendencies on these three polarities. For example, one person might be a thinking-intuition-introvert type. Another individual might be a feeling-sensation-extrovert type.

The Cayce readings do not refer to the same blueprint for measuring temperament. Instead they offer a model based on astrology. However, Cayce's astrology was not the popular approach that is available on the newsstand today. The so-called sun signs method has gained widespread notoriety; virtually every teenager and adult knows whether he or she is an Aquarius, Taurus, Capricorn, or some other sign. Actually, the twelve zodiacal constellations offer yet another system of describing temperament. The method is ancient and probably contains considerable wisdom, but unfortunately, our modern tendency has been to dismiss some of astrology's more subtle, esoteric meanings and commercialize its basic ideas (e.g., predictive horoscopes in the morning newspaper, coffee cups with your name and sun sign, and so forth).

However, the Cayce readings rarely refer to sun signs. Instead, the astrological focus is on the planets. In almost every life reading, Cayce provided the recipient with an analysis of temperament based on the symbology of the planets. Usually about three particular planets were described as being most influential on the soul for the present lifetime. So whereas Jung might have labeled someone's temperament as feeling-intuition-extroversion, Cayce might have defined someone else's in terms of Mercury, Mars, and Neptune, for example.

What are we to make of the system used in the Cayce readings? How can we interpret the significance of the planets?

Contemporary students of Cayce's astrology material generally agree that he was identifying eight critical dimensions that might play a role in shaping one's temperament. For most people about three planets were sufficient to present a picture. The factors and their symbolic labels are as follows:

Mercury: Tendency to intellectualize and analyze; a quick mind; likes to get to the facts.

Venus: Prefers to do things in partnership; appreciates the beauty of people and places; vulnerable.

Mars: Likes competition, challenge, and activities that demand physical energy; tendency toward anger.

Jupiter: Relates to large endeavors; likes philosophy and getting the big picture; comfortable with power and money; expansive and liberal.

Saturn: Conservative, cautious, and reluctant to change (ironically, this often causes sudden changes in life experience); disciplined and persistent.

Uranus: Swings from one extreme to the other in mood or emotion; high-strung; scientific and inventive; highly intuitive or psychic.

Neptune: Attracted to the mysterious; mystical, idealistic, otherworldly, and devotional; attracted to the sea and other forces of nature.

Pluto: Combustive, explosive, passionate, and self-centered. (Modern astronomers prefer to label Pluto as a dwarf planet and not a full-fledged member of the solar system's planets. However, in Cayce's era astronomers thought otherwise, and it was an element of his temperament schema.)

No matter what system you prefer for defining your character, remember this principle: Your basic temperament doesn't define your talents and abilities so much as it provides a context in which these assets operate. Neither does your temperament type designate your soul's destiny. It may, however, provide some clues about the settings and environments in which you are most likely to feel at home and productive—clues that could be valuable in choosing a career path. In fact, one vocational guidance researcher, John Holland, has developed an elaborate job-search method that is based on this very assumption: *Your most fulfilling occupation is probably one in which the work environment matches your temperament.* Let's examine the highlights of his approach.

The Holland Method for Vocational Choices

Holland uses the word *disposition* rather than *temperament*, but it denotes the same concept. In his classic book, *Making Vocational Choices*, he puts it this way: "A person's interests and competencies create a particular personal disposition that leads him to think, perceive, and act in special ways."* Whereas Cayce defines eight temperamental types and Jung suggests three pairs of polar opposites, Holland proposes six personality types: realistic, investigative, artistic, social, enterprising, and conventional. Looking at the characteristics of each type in the following pages, you may recognize certain overlaps with Cayce's planetary types. In spite of some similarities, there is probably

---

* John Holland, *Making Vocational Choices*, 2nd edition (Englewood Cliffs, NJ: Prentice-Hall, 1985), p. 2.

not an exact fit. The most important parallel is that both Cayce and Holland recognized that temperament type plays a key role in helping an individual see his or her best vocation, something that will provide meaning and fulfillment.

Both sources also observe that very few people are pure types. Cayce's life readings usually refer to three planets to adequately capture the temperament. Holland suggests that each of us has a disposition profile or personality pattern that can be described with the three most prominent types. For example, consider the three-part Holland code identifier "RIC," or realistic-investigative-conventional. This temperament most closely fits the characteristics of the realistic type. The second-most prominent type in this temperament is investigative, and the third-most prominent is the conventional type.

However, not only do individual people have a disposition, so do groupings of people. Each work environment can be categorized by the same six types, or even by a profile that describes the three most salient ones. For example, one company may create a social-enterprising-artistic type of work setting. That flavor is created by the types of people who are dominant and the kinds of opportunities offered in that workplace. Holland's approach to finding the right career is based on the idea that you must find a work environment that matches your personal disposition type, because there you will find the opportunities and rewards that you need.

All of this seems to make sense, but the obvious question remains, "How can I determine which type I am? What is my temperament profile?" Holland has an elaborate method involving questionnaires, inventories, and interviews. No doubt that is the best and most reliable way to do it. Never-theless, for many people some commonsense self-analysis may yield almost as accurate a reading. Study the descriptions of each temperament type that follows and compare them to your own traits. No single type is likely to describe you perfectly, so be prepared to select a mix of the three that match you best, in order of how closely they fit.

The realistic type (R). This temperament style is also sometimes called "doers," and it's oriented toward systematic, ordered ways of dealing with physical life on concrete, here-and-now terms. It tends to be associated with mechanical or athletic abilities. This sort of person often values objective things or tangible characteristics such as money, power, and status. The mirror opposite of this temperament is the social type; the realistic type usually shies away from the demands of human relations. The realistic person may have some or all of these qualities: detached, frank, genuine, materialistic, practical, thrifty, narrow-minded. Among the occupations for which "R" is the primary Holland code are mechanical engineer, graphic arts technician, cabinetmaker, machinist, appliance repairer, airline pilot, forester, auditor, technical writer, and floral designer. These are, of course, just ten out of literally hundreds of occupations that have "R" as the primary Holland code. The same will be true of the tiny sampling of occupations that are listed as examples for the other five types.

The investigative type (I). This disposition is sometimes called "thinkers," and it's directed toward observation and exploration of life in order to understand it and control it. It tends to be linked to skills with mathematics and science. This type of person is often scholarly or particularly self-confident about his or her intellectual grasp of things. The polar opposite of this disposition is the enterprising type; therefore the investigative type is usually lacking in leadership abilities and persuasion skills. This sort of person is likely to possess some of these traits: analytical, cautious, curious, intellectual, introspective, precise, reserved. Among the occupations for which "I" is the primary Holland code are aeronautical engineer, physician, taxi driver, navigator, architect, sociologist, pharmacist, physicist, laboratory assistant, and land surveyor.

The artistic type (A). This temperament style is sometimes called "creators," and it's oriented toward free, unrestricted activities that create art forms or products. It tends to be associated with skills in language, art, music, drama, and writing. This sort of person usually values aesthetic qualities and is likely to be intuitive, nonconforming, and disorganized. The mirror opposite of this temperament is the conventional type; therefore the artistic type is probably uncomfortable with systematic, orderly activities or business machines. The artistic person may have some or all of these characteristics: complicated, emotional, idealistic, imaginative, impractical, impulsive, original. Among the occupations for which "A" is the primary Holland code are cake decorator, landscape architect, clothes designer, playwright, critic, music teacher, news editor, illustrator, psychic reader, and personnel manager.

The social type (S). This disposition is also known as "helpers," and it's directed toward human relations, working with others to train, inform, or assist people. It tends to be linked to skills with interpersonal situations and teaching. The social type usually values societal and ethical ideals. The polar opposite of this disposition is the realistic type; therefore the social type is usually lacking in mechanical and pragmatic skills. This sort of person is likely to possess some of these traits: cooperative, friendly, generous, kind, responsible, tactful, understanding. Among the occupations for which "S" is the primary Holland code are hospital orderly, mail carrier, athletic coach, clinical psychologist, institution director, counselor, hairstylist, nurse, elementary school teacher, and disc jockey.

The enterprising type (E). This temperament style is sometimes called "persuaders," and it's oriented toward organizational goals and economic gain. It tends to be associated with skills in leadership, initiative, and persuasion. This sort of person usually values political and financial achievement, and is likely to be adventurous, energetic, and self-confident. The mirror opposite of this temperament is the investigative type; therefore the enterprising type is probably uncomfortable with scientific, mathematical issues or with situations that require patient, careful observation. The enterprising person may have some or all of these characteristics: acquisitive, ambitious, argumentative, domineering, impulsive, optimistic, talkative. Among the occupations for which "E" is the primary Holland code are maintenance superintendent, dispatcher, insurance sales agent, bellhop, clown, reporter, flight attendant, real estate agent, health club manager, and tax attorney.

The conventional type (C). This disposition is also known as "organizers," and it's directed toward assembling information and things into reliable, stable patterns. It tends to be linked with skills of record keeping, business demands, and clerical or computational duties. The conventional type usually values commercial and economic achievements. The polar opposite of this disposition is the artistic type; therefore the conventional type usually feels an aversion to aesthetic, free, unsystematized activities. This sort of person is likely to possess some of these traits: conforming, conscientious, efficient, obedient, orderly, persistent, practical. Among the occupations for which "C" is the primary Holland code are restaurant server, payroll clerk, secretary, medical records technician, cashier, building inspector, financial analyst, electronics assembler, bookkeeper, and proofreader.

Holland's six types offer a fascinating model but appear to be highly speculative. Does any independent evidence support his theory? Are these six descriptions the best way to "slice the pie" of human character traits? A least one autonomous researcher arrived at similar conclusions using highly sophisticated statistical analysis. Working in the early 1950s, an independent investigator named J. P. Guilford applied a technique known as factor analysis to a mountain of data concerning human interests. The big picture he was able to portray shows that six major groupings, or factors, emerge from the assessment. Guilford named them mechanical, scientific, aesthetic, social welfare, business, and clerical. These results virtually restate Holland's six types: realistic, investigative, artistic, social, enterprising, and conventional.

Do any of these types sound like you? Since you have many sub-personalities—many distinct identities or I's—you may find yourself easily relating to almost all six of the types. However, try to recognize which temperament or set of temperaments fits your most essential self. At the core of who you know yourself to be, which one matches you best?

One of the most useful aspects of the Holland system is what you can do with your code. Remember his theory that you're most likely to find career satisfaction in work environments that correspond to your own temperament. Take a best guess at your three-letter Holland Code. Think of which of the six dispositional types sounds most like you; then, what is second-most; and finally, third-most. That gives you a three-part Holland Code. Then visit O*NET at https://www .onetonline.org/explore/interests/ to look at examples of occupations that fit well with your code. It can be a great way to brainstorm options if you are thinking about switching careers or if you are an emergent adult just deciding on a first career. Enter either your top three dispositions or (to get a considerably wider list of possibilities) just your top two dispositional types. It can be almost as much fun as getting a clairvoyant reading from someone as gifted as Cayce!

Epilogue

THE CHAPTERS OF this book have been a journey in themselves. They serve as a road map or guidebook for charting a course in self-discovery. And it's a journey that you probably will want to take more than once. We are continually finding, at ever deeper and more subtle levels, our purpose in life. We are continually discovering ways to live and fulfill that purpose, our mission, with greater engagement and broader outreach. This really is a lifelong endeavor, and we often stand in need of renewal and reinspiration. This may well be a book to which you will return from time to time in the years ahead.

There is perhaps no better way to conclude this book than a story from the Cayce archives. It's the stories of real-life people who were helped by Cayce that make his philosophy come alive for us decades later. The challenges that were faced by people in the 1930s and 1940s, when Cayce gave most of his life readings, are tests that people still face today. Almost ninety years may have gone by, but the human condition is still the same. We are born with aptitudes and gifts. We have life experiences that tend to cover them or divert us from claiming them. We long for something more than mundane life seems to be offering us, and there is the urge to wake up and remember what we are called to do in life. Here's one man's story.

The Story of One Man's Search

It was the summer of 1929, the twilight of the Roaring Twenties in America. Although few suspected it, an extraordinary economic calamity loomed just a few months ahead: the Great Depression.

But that summer was still full of hope and promise for any energetic, bright young person. In mid-August a man of thirty-two ventured from his home in Massachusetts to Virginia Beach, Virginia. He traveled to meet a remarkable person with a reputation for helping people with their most perplexing problems. The man had heard about Edgar Cayce from a friend and had learned how Cayce could put himself into a sleeplike trance state in which great wisdom flowed. The man took the long journey hoping to get answers from Cayce for some tough questions about what to do with his life.

As a man of thirty-two, he was at an age where most of his friends were already settled into a career and a traditional lifestyle. His companions from college years were married; many of them now had children too. They all seemed fairly happy—or at least established in a steady routine.

But this man was different. Maybe he was restless. Or maybe he was unwilling to get fixed in a way of life that fulfilled everyone else's expectations but didn't satisfy his. He was employed as a teacher of accounting, but he sensed that there were other, greater purposes for his life.

He had written ahead to Cayce requesting a psychic reading and had been given an appointment for August 12. The friend who recommended Cayce had suggested the man try to be present for the reading. Most people didn't go to such trouble and were satisfied with receiving a typed transcript of the entranced Cayce's words. But this man made the trip.

He arrived at the Cayce home, located just a few hundred yards from the Atlantic Ocean. He was greeted by Edgar and his wife, Gertrude, and Cayce's secretary, Gladys, who lived there as part of the family. After a short time to get acquainted, they all went back into Cayce's study, where his psychic readings were given. Two striking features of the room caught the man's eye. The first was a large bulletin board covered with photographs, faces of people Cayce loved and had helped through his readings. The second was a couch where Cayce would recline and put himself into the altered state of consciousness required for his clairvoyant work.

That afternoon disappointed the man. Cayce was unable to give a reading for him. Later he was told this did not happen often, but there were occasions when Cayce was not able to reach the state from which his information came. They would try again. The next day would not be convenient, but the reading was rescheduled for August 14.

Now the man had two extra days to consider Edgar Cayce and what had happened so far. The more he thought, the more his initial disappointment turned to gratefulness and respect. He felt relief to see firsthand that Cayce was not perfect. Clearly he was not dealing with a god, but an ordinary man who did extraordinary things. And as with any ordinary man, there were some days when he wasn't up to his full potential. Furthermore, this experience helped the man see Cayce's integrity. Rather than fake a reading, he had been humble enough to admit failure and ask for another chance.

They tried again on the afternoon of the 14th, and this time Cayce was successful. A life reading was given, a type of psychic discourse that was still relatively novel for Cayce. In fact, for the first twenty-two years of his clairvoyant work—from 1901 to 1923—the only kind of reading he had known he could give was for health problems. These physical readings were the source of his notoriety, and in the summer of 1929 there was a small but thriving hospital in Virginia Beach that treated patients on the basis of their health readings. The medical staff carefully followed the clairvoyant diagnoses and holistic treatment regimens prescribed in the readings.

However, the life reading given for this man did not concern his physical health. Instead it offered him wise spiritual counseling about his purpose in life. Like an insightful, loving parent, Cayce's psychic source helped him to recognize some of his most important talents and strengths: an aptitude for mathematical calculations, strong desires to study and learn, and a deep interest in people. On the other hand, certain weaknesses were described: a tendency to show affection only rarely and a certain way of acting that other people often mistook for fatalism.

The reading also described several past lifetimes in which some of these talents and weaknesses had been developed. Reincarnation may have been a foreign notion to the man, but it was presented in the reading without apology. He was told of a lifetime during the Crusades and of another in the time of Jesus.

And then, perhaps the most interesting and useful, he was given suggestions about occupations in which he was likely to achieve success: architecture, aeronautics, and astronomy. Two nontraditional career possibilities were also offered: numerology and astrology.

However, the most important thing given to the young man that summer afternoon by Cayce's life reading was a clear statement of his soul's purpose. For just a moment, seeing beyond the specifics of certain job possibilities, the reading described what this man, this soul, was truly *gifted* to do in life. It called him to remember his authentic vocation: to help and guide others to see the spiritual meaning in numbers. The reading described how mathematics and numbers are one way in which universal laws and spiritual truths can be expressed. It invited the man to a lifelong adventure to benefit himself and others by fully making use of this innate gift. It might be done through a career using the mathematical and geometric precision required of an architect or aeronautical engineer. Or the life mission of this soul might be lived through a job in astronomy, in which the mathematical orderliness of the universe is discovered. The reading also prompted him to fulfill part of his purpose in life through an activity such as numerology or astrology. He was even encouraged to become the astrologer for Edgar Cayce's own organization.

For thirty minutes this man sat in Edgar Cayce's study and listened to an amazing description of his life and its highest purpose. In just half an hour his life was changed.

He visited the Cayce Hospital and spent some time alone with Edgar Cayce before returning home to Massachusetts. This unusual man with the mysterious psychic powers was not at all aloof to the people he offered to help. In fact, after tapping the depths of universal wisdom and soul memory, Cayce took the young man out fishing! Two weeks later, Cayce received this letter of appreciation:

Please send me half a dozen or so of each of the booklets published by your Association, so that I may use them among my friends with whom I have talked regarding your work. I look back with genuine pleasure on my trip to Virginia Beach and know that the friendships that resulted will always be with me.

I am working out a plan of study, in fact have already started the study of astronomy and astrology, as suggested in my life reading. I am tremendously interested in the work that the Association is doing and know that its unselfish motive and ideals will bear fruit.

Does my fishing record still stand? If anyone catches a larger fish I'll know it is one of those I lost off my hook.

I send my best wishes to you and your family and ask that you remember me to them and to my friends at the Hospital (256-1).

The story of this man is one of hundreds from the Cayce files. But those archival records are only one part of the Cayce legacy. Just as important is your own story! The legacy of these teachings Cayce gave in the first half of the twentieth century extends now into the twenty-first century. The way you take hold of these principles and exercises about finding and living your mission creates a narrative just as revealing and hopeful as this story from 1929. Try writing a few sentences in your story today. Find some small step on the journey of discovering and living your mission, and take that step right now.

APPENDIX I

A Theory of Creation

One of the oldest religious questions asks, "How were we created? What brought humanity into being?" For centuries the greatest minds of theology and philosophy have proposed explanations. The Edgar Cayce readings suggest an answer that is yet another attempt to give greater meaning to our lives today by describing the original purpose for humanity.

Ultimately the problem of creation cannot be solved. Our analytical minds, functioning in the familiar framework of time and space, probably cannot grasp the complexities and higher states of consciousness that were involved in the authentic story. The source of the Cayce readings recognized that limitation. It appreciated the restrictions of our logical thinking but still found a way to present the essential themes of creation. For example, even though God is not a superperson, we may be able to gain an approximate understanding of certain divine qualities by referring to the best human qualities.

The readings present the saga of creation and the evolution of souls as a myth. Remember that the deepest meaning of myth is not misconception or falsehood. Unfortunately in colloquial language of recent times, that is what the word has come to connote. Actually myth communicates a truth that is so profound and important that it can't be captured in logical terms. Myth makes use of images, metaphors, and symbols in a story line that teaches your head as well as your heart. Whenever you encounter a myth, pay attention to both the new thoughts and the new feelings it awakens in you. It's a powerful way to learn, and many people best understand the meaning of life through this approach.

The Bible influenced Cayce's thinking and helped to shape the mythic account of our origins that he gave. Anyone who studies transcripts of his psychic readings notices that the language is stylistically similar to that in the King James Bible and that the readings frequently refer to scriptural stories. What may not be as well known is that in his normal, conscious life, Edgar Cayce was an avid reader of both the Old and New Testaments. Fulfilling a promise that he had made as a boy, he read the entire Bible once for every year of his life—every word sixty-seven times!

The Cayce readings built upon the basic account in Genesis but gave additional facts and interpreted many biblical passages in their broader and more symbolic intent. According to the readings, there is no doubt that we were created by God. Physical evolution of the human body is a fact as well, but it can't explain our inner, spiritual nature.

The readings began with a question that is most fundamental: Why did God create us? The problems of how and when are not nearly so crucial as the purpose for which the Creator brought us into being. The meaning of our lives today is shaped by this primal intention. The initial purpose was companionship. God desired companionship.

This makes God sound like a lonely old man in the sky, but remember that the Cayce readings present this explanation as a myth. The desire for companionship is another way of saying that the spiritual forces of the universe are motivated to seek *loving relationship*. Something about the nature of God has an impulse toward connection. And we were created to be a step toward relationship, connection, companionship, and love. This gives us a first clue about the meaning of life in our modern world. Purpose and fulfillment are most likely to be found by making loving connections with other living things around us.

After addressing that fundamental question, the Cayce readings tackle the more complex issues of how we as souls have evolved over the centuries and how we came to be here on the earth. Our creation as souls was in the spiritual realm and only later did we come into physical bodies. Cayce's mythic account of souls and their journey in consciousness is complicated and often enigmatic. Many longtime students of this material believe that the readings given on this subject are the most difficult to interpret and understand. Briefly, however, here is the story that we might extract from a careful probe. It revolves around three great themes: two kinds of perfection, the problem of good and evil, and the struggle between freedom and destiny.

In the beginning—not a certain number of years ago, but beyond the realm of time as we understand it—God created us as souls. Each of us was given three attributes: spirit, mind, and free will. The spirit is the very essence of the life force that animates us. It is that core of our being that is immortal. Mind is the creative power within us. With the mind we are cocreators with God and able to shape our own realities. The saying "Thoughts are things" reflects that fact. Finally, free will makes us independent. How could God ever have created us to be companions if we were merely robots who were blindly obedient to his every wish? Genuine relationship demands autonomy. And so, at creation we were given our independence: free will.

In our original state we were perfect and experienced oneness with God. It might be said that he looked upon us and was pleased. However, mingled with that pleasure was a desire for something more. What more could there be? Perfect is perfect, right? And if we were already one with God, what further development was possible?

Perhaps we can best look at these questions with an analogy. A newborn baby might be called perfect. With his innocence, openness, and spontaneity, a newborn is a wonder to behold. And if we speculate about his state of consciousness, we might conclude that he still experiences a sense of oneness with his mother. Even after the umbilical cord has been severed, it often appears that the newborn is still psychically connected with his mother.

The point of this analogy is the relative meaning of two words: *perfection* and *oneness*. The kind of perfection seen in a newborn is not the ultimate human perfection. Obviously the newborn lacks experience and has not even begun to express some of the highest human qualities such as kindness, self-sacrifice, and creativity. Later as an adult, he may strive for a mature ideal of perfection.

In a similar way the oneness that fills the mind of a newborn is not the oneness that is experienced by a spiritually enlightened adult. The difference is the infant does not yet know his own individuality. He feels a oneness unconscious of itself. On the other hand, the enlightened adult is filled with a conscious oneness that knows universality and individuality at the same time.

This distinction helps us understand how Cayce defined the purpose and plan God had for our growth and development: to know ourselves to be ourselves yet also one with the universe. At creation we were perfect in one way, but God desired that we would attain a more mature perfection. Real companionship and relationship would be possible only after that development. At creation we had a kind of oneness, but it was unconscious—a sort of oceanic oneness in which we did not know consciously our own unique individuality. It was the plan of our Creator that we would evolve in consciousness to experience a higher order of oneness.

Of course the issue of individuality sounds paradoxical. If initially we were given the gift of free will, then it could be argued that a sense of our independence was available all along. The catch is even though we were given free will, we didn't at first make full use of it. Metaphorically we might say at creation the will was still sleeping within the soul and only later did it begin to awaken.

Consider this analogy. Suppose a friend gives you a beautifully gift-wrapped birthday present. From the moment it's in your possession the gift is fully yours, even though you haven't yet unwrapped it. At the appropriate time you'll untie the ribbon and remove the colorful paper, revealing the exact nature of the present. The gift was yours from the moment it came into your hands, but now that its precise identity is known, you can do something with it.

The same themes were at work in our spiritual creation. God gave each of us freedom of will. From the beginning we have been individual souls, but at first we were not able to make use of our autonomy and specialness. We were unconscious; our free will was like a present waiting to be unwrapped and used.

However, God had a plan to change this. According to Cayce's mythic account of our origins, souls began a long journey to become conscious companions with the Creator. Something was required if we were to develop and unfold spiritually. We needed to experience more directly our own individuality, and that could happen only if we separated ourselves from the sense of oneness and universality.

In God's plan we were led into more limited dimensions of consciousness, places in awareness where our immature individuality would not be overwhelmed by infinite states of mind. Many kinds of experience in many different dimensions were prepared for us, only one of which was the three-dimensional consciousness we know now as the material life of the earth. In other words, physical experience was one place that God had in mind for us because of the opportunities for growth it can provide.

Cayce's mythic story even gives a name to one soul who led us into the earthly adventure. He was called Amelius. As strange as that name may sound, it resembles another word, *ameliorate*, which means "to make something better; to improve upon." We might interpret this to say long, long ago we were part of a great movement of spiritual beings who came into this three-dimensional world. We entered because there was great opportunity and purpose here, and we were led by an impulse to become even better than we were when God created us.

What was the opportunity offered by physical experience? In this dimension we have a special chance to make use of free will. Something about material consciousness gives the will a possibility to awaken. However, an obvious temptation stood in the way. God's plan wouldn't be fulfilled if we misused our freedom once we entered this dimension of awareness. Independence leaves room for rebellion, and that's exactly what happened. Perhaps some measure of rebellion was inevitable. That's how any free being tests limits and boundaries. The problem came when souls continued with their rebellion and began to waste the opportunity for spiritual development.

This mythic tale narrated in the Cayce readings is very abstract and philosophical. You may wonder how it could help you find meaning for your life in today's world, but maybe the question of independence is not so far removed from your immediate experience. Do you remember what it was like to break free from your childhood family and become your own person? The analogy best fits someone whose early home life was generally harmonious and supportive. Imagine a young person, just reaching the adolescent years, who finds it hard to separate herself enough to find her own values and goals in life. However, something in her knows the separation is necessary. As long as her thoughts and feelings revolve around those of her parents, she never becomes her own person. As long as she stays in the cocoon of her childhood home, she never tests her own wings and learns to fly.

Perhaps in her teenage years this hypothetical girl will have some rebellious episodes. Hopefully they won't harm her or others. During those years she may also be successful in finding constructive ways to assert her independence and need for separation. It may be difficult for her parents because they feel rejected, but if they truly love her, they know how valuable it is for their daughter to discover her will and really come to know her own identity. God loved us that much and still does. We are given the freedom to use or misuse our independence.

Unfortunately most souls began long ago to distort the meaning of physical life, and they have continued to do so. In Cayce's saga he described how spiritual beings came into the third dimension for a clear purpose but then diverted themselves from that purpose. The mission we all shared when we entered material experience can be characterized by these words: to bring the infinite into the finite. We each bear within us the spiritual essence of our Creator: the infinite and universal. Our mission is to discover how these divine qualities can be expressed in a focused, individualized way, in a finite, physical life. It's a tremendous challenge, but when we are successful, we become conscious, cocreative companions with God.

What does all this tell us about the value of physical life? Some religious traditions teach that material existence is a tragic error or a cosmic illusion. Cayce stated the opposite in his story of creation. Our lives in the physical world are of the greatest possible value. God not only respects and honors our individuality, but he also prepared this experience in materiality for us because of its opportunity for spiritual growth. Things in human history have often gone wrong, but they don't have to continue that way.

What can we do to help things move in the direction of spiritual development? A good start is to take a closer look at how things got off track thousands of years ago. The Cayce story provides a fascinating description of how souls chose to divert themselves from their original mission in the earth. The essential problem came from the way we decided to use the powers of mind and free will.

First we discovered the extraordinary creative power of the mind. We played with our ability to shape physical reality with our thoughts. Nowadays we hear the saying "Thoughts are things," but thousands of years ago that truth was experienced vividly. By mentally focusing on a desire, we could quickly make it into a physical reality. This condition is remembered today in legends about a genie who can grant any wish. This magical character symbolizes the creative power of the mind itself. But remember what always happens in such tales: The wishes are granted and they get the recipient into trouble. If the number of wishes is limited, then invariably the last wish must be saved to undo all the problems created by the other wishes.

How did our desires lead us astray? Many of them were selfish. They focused on things that led to personal pleasure but didn't reflect our higher, spiritual nature. God planned for us to use the mind and will to bring qualities such as love, beauty, and truth into physical expression. However, that required a concern for ourselves *and* for others. We became preoccupied with ourselves and developed a will to private fulfillment. In other words, the great possibilities for the individual self got lost in selfishness. We forgot the work of loving and helping each other, and then we began to forget the spiritual realm to which we also belong.

In the story from the Cayce readings, God did not give up on any of us after just one lifetime. Upon the death of the physical body, each soul temporarily left the material dimension and once again entered the spiritual world. However, the soul carried with it all its mental patterns of confusion and selfishness. Obviously none of us were yet fit to be called companions of God. Rather than judge us once and for all, God offered us additional chances. When the time was right, we were allowed to come again into the physical world—born once more in human form through a process called reincarnation.

A Parable of the Meaning of Life

Stories make things easier to remember; they also touch us at levels of understanding deeper than the intellect. Perhaps that's why some of the greatest spiritual teachers used fables, myths, and parables to make their points.

Let's translate some of the abstract concepts of this appendix into images that are simple but potent. In the form of a parable we can capture the essential themes of the purpose of life and the mission we all share. It's the tale of Pinocchio, a well-known legend that has been reinterpreted by that master mythmaker of the twentieth century, Walt Disney.

As you read the following synopsis of the plot, think of Pinocchio as a symbol of the human soul on its journey of spiritual evolution. His story is your story. Pinocchio is created by the influence of two characters, one male and one female, just as the Cayce readings sometimes refer to "Mother-Father God." First Pinocchio is carved by the kindly wood craftsman, Geppetto. Then the Blue Fairy pays a visit during the night and with a tap of her magic wand bestows the gift of life. At the same time, she chooses an unsuspecting cricket named Jiminy and gives him a mission: to stay close to Pinocchio and be his conscience. This is reminiscent of something found in the Cayce readings about our creation: God placed within the unconscious mind of every soul the consciousness of truth.

When Geppetto wakes up the next morning he is overjoyed. There is a celebration to honor the new life of Pinocchio. However, the more Geppetto thinks about it, the clearer he becomes about his greatest desire. He wishes Pinocchio might become a real boy.

Knowing that his wish can be fulfilled only if Pinocchio learns and grows, Geppetto sends his son off to school. In a very significant scene, Pinocchio is led out the front door by his father. He is sent off on a purposeful journey accompanied only by his friend Jiminy Cricket. Pinocchio does not run away from home. His departure is with his father's blessing and its purpose is Pinocchio's own improvement. He is on an adventure to achieve amelioration, to become something better—a real boy.

However, once he is out in the world, problems begin. Using his newfound freedom, Pinocchio makes some bad choices. He confronts temptation in the form of Honest John, the evil fox. Jiminy Cricket protests but to no avail. First Pinocchio succumbs to the temptation of pride. He follows the lead of Honest John and joins a carnival troupe. He performs to great acclaim as the dancing marionette who needs no strings. Sadly the fame can be enjoyed only in small doses. Between performances he is locked in a cage, and it is only when the Blue Fairy intervenes with her powers of grace that he is set free and given another chance. Before his release, however, Pinocchio has the embarrassing experience of his nose growing longer whenever he lies to the Blue Fairy. Lying is symptomatic of the evil influencing Pinocchio. In fact, in his study of the nature of evil, *People of the Lie*, M. Scott Peck calls lying the central feature by which we can recognize evil. Ultimately we can't hide the source of our motives;

it's written in our faces. For Pinocchio this takes an exaggerated, symbolic form with the length of his nose.

Jiminy Cricket is determined to help Pinocchio stay on track this time, but before long additional temptations arise. Honest John appears again, this time with an offer that's hard to refuse. Pinocchio is invited to Pleasure Island, a place where boys can have fun all day and indulge all their appetites. Jiminy Cricket knows nothing good can come from such a place, but Pinocchio ignores his advice. Soon he's having a great time on this island of amusements and candy.

Pleasure Island, of course, is symbolic of our own self-indulgent materialism. What happens to Pinocchio and all the other boys if they linger there too long? They begin to turn into animals—donkeys, to be exact. The jackass is quite a fitting image for the state to which we as souls fell. We forgot who we were and what our mission was, just as Pinocchio lost sight of why Geppetto sent him off.

As Pinocchio notices that he is growing long ears and a tail, he turns to Jiminy Cricket and begs for help. There is still time to escape. Pinocchio's "repentance" pays off because Jiminy Cricket knows the way to get off the island. Once they are away from the immediate danger, they begin to search for Geppetto. But where is he? They return to his home and discover that he has gone out looking for Pinocchio himself. This image is particularly important for us. It suggests that not only are we seeking God, but God is also searching for us.

Pinocchio receives guidance indicating the whereabouts of his father. He can be found deep beneath the sea in the belly of the great whale Monstro. Geppetto's boat has been swallowed by this "great fish." Admittedly a whale is a mammal and not a fish, but if we stretch the facts slightly, it suggests an interesting interpretation. A fish is an ancient symbol for the reconciliation of spirit and matter. The sea is a symbol of the unconscious. And so where will Pinocchio find what he seeks? Where will we find the object of our spiritual longing? Within our own unconscious selves. Our true spiritual nature resides there.

As Pinocchio and Jiminy Cricket search the sea for Geppetto, they are luckily swallowed by the same whale. A joyful reunion between Pinocchio and his father takes place in the belly of Monstro. However, they soon realize their predicament. Somehow they must escape and bring their reunion back to the light of day and dry land. In other words, our spiritual journey doesn't end when we begin to reencounter our spiritual depths in dreams, prayer, or meditation. The next step is to bring that higher state of consciousness into daily life, and that is often the most difficult task.

In the parable Pinocchio has a plan. He devises a way for them to escape, but it requires great strength and courage. At one point it appears Geppetto might drown, so Pinocchio sacrifices himself to save his father. When Geppetto regains consciousness on the beach, he sees beside him the lifeless body of his son. Grieving deeply, he takes the body home and lays it on a bed. To his surprise the Blue Fairy returns and once again touches Pinocchio with her wand. He is resurrected and thus fulfills his mission, coming back to life as a real boy.

This parable of our own journey in spiritual development tells parts of the story that we haven't yet fulfilled. You may wonder where you are in the story. You can find yourself at many points. You probably spend some of each day in the consciousness symbolized by Pleasure Island. You may have some moments of consciously trying to get off the island or times when you are looking for your own Geppetto. No matter what part of this mythic story seems to fit you most often, the good news is the ending.

This is the meaning of life: We are in the process of becoming conscious, cocreative companions with God. The blossoming of our real nature may still be far off, but we can do things every day that take us a step in that direction. The purpose of life we all share is making the infinite finite—bringing spiritual qualities into individual expression.

The Theory of Reincarnation

The idea that every soul is born with a mission does *not* require a belief in reincarnation. We might suppose, for example, that an individual soul, along with its sense of unique purposefulness, is created at about the same time as the biological conception of the body it will occupy. However, this materialistic view is not the perspective found in the Cayce readings. Instead, we are invited to consider the hypothesis of reincarnation: a theory of rebirth that implies that many of the tools for fulfilling a life's mission (as well as obstacles that could frustrate it) have their origin in previous lives on earth. Reincarnation is both a controversial subject and an ancient one. It is most readily associated with philosophies and religions of the East. But many examples of it exist in esoteric Western thought, and even today there is a growing acceptance of the notion in our modern society. For example, a poll conducted by the Pew Research Center in 2009 found that

24 percent of the public overall and 22 percent of Christians say they believe in reincarnation.

Of course, the word *reincarnation* often connotes a variety of ideas. But for purposes of our study, it will simply mean a theory of human rebirth that states that after physical death a soul may return in human form, carrying with it predispositions of temperament, interest, talent, and even physical tendencies. This notion is only theoretical and probably will never be provable to everyone's satisfaction. As we shall soon see, there is evidence—often very startling—to support the concept, but there always seems to be an alternative way of explaining it. For example, even the most remarkable and best-documented cases of "remembered past lives" could be explained as telepathy or clairvoyance. However, we are then left with a problem at least as mysterious and difficult: how to explain the workings of ESP.

For many people the idea of reincarnation is foreign or unattractive. In fact, when the concept first began to come through his readings, Edgar Cayce himself rejected the notion. He had never seen any reference to it in the Bible, so he was inclined to denounce it. It was only after many years of careful study and soul-searching that he came to accept the theory.

Reincarnation may or may not make sense to you. It is not a required belief in order to work with the approaches found in this book. Nevertheless, many people find the idea helpful, and they believe there is evidence that supports the theory. The most remarkable cases are probably those in which characteristics of the physical body seem to carry over. For example, a few cases suggest a birthmark may be related to a physical trauma in the preceding lifetime. Dr. Ian Stevenson, of the University of Virginia School of Medicine, conducted extensive research on this subject spanning more than forty years. His investigations of evidence for reincarnation focused on children who claim to have conscious memories of a past life. For several of those young people, the details of the past-life story match a birthmark on the current body. Many of Stevenson's best cases come from the Tlingit (pronounced "Klingit") Indians of southeastern Alaska. They believe in reincarnation, and this belief has a strong influence on their religious and social behaviors.

One case, taken from Dr. Stevenson's classic book, *Twenty Cases Suggestive of Reincarnation*, concerned a man named Victor Vincent, who died in the spring of 1946. According to details Stevenson gathered later, Vincent had grown especially close to his niece during the last year of his life. He even told her, "I'm coming back as your next son. I hope I don't stutter then as much as I do now. Your son will have these scars." He proceeded to show his niece and her husband two scars from surgical operations, one on his back and one on his nose.

About eighteen months after Vincent's death, the niece gave birth to a son who had two marks on his body exactly like the scars of his deceased great uncle. Although Dr. Stevenson did not learn of this case and examine the boy until he was fifteen years old, the mark on his back especially seemed to resemble the kind that comes from surgery.

Stevenson also learned of some fascinating events in the boy's early childhood. When he was thirteen months old and just learning to talk, his mother tried to teach him to respond with his name when he was asked for it. Once he replied, "Don't you know me. I'm Kahkody," which was the tribal name of the deceased uncle, Victor.

At the ages of two and three the boy also recognized and identified family members of Victor Vincent's without any coaching from his parents. Later in his early childhood he was able to tell stories about events that had happened to him in the previous life as Victor, stories that the family confirmed. However, around the age of nine he began to make fewer and fewer statements about this past life, and by the time Stevenson met him when he was fifteen, he had no recollection of Victor.

As a scientific investigator, Stevenson was careful not to make any claims of proof of reincarnation. However, the evidence is highly suggestive and illustrates how some aspects of soul memory may work. Stevenson retired in 2002 and passed away in 2007, but the work he began continues at the Division of Perceptual Studies at the University of Virginia. Dr. Jim Tucker now directs those efforts, and his published books include *Life Before Life: A Scientific Investigation of Children's Memories of Previous Lives* (2005) and *Return to Life: Extraordinary Cases of Children Who Remember Past Lives* (2013). The *Virginia Magazine* published a cover story in 2013 about Tucker's work entitled "The Science of Reincarnation." An electronic copy of the article is available at http://uvamagazine.org/articles/the_science_of_reincarnation.

Hundreds of readings by Edgar Cayce provide another source of evidence for reincarnation, although it's of a different variety than Stevenson's and Tucker's work. Cayce gave more than nineteen hundred past-life readings. Each one included a lengthy section that analyzed current personality traits in light of hypothetical past lives. In many of the cases we find convincing stories that help explain problems and positive opportunities.

But how important is reincarnation to the Cayce philosophy? The answer is paradoxical: It is simultaneously very important and almost inconsequential. How can we have it both ways? Only by distinguishing between the underlying principles that govern reincarnation and a personal belief in the theory. The principles—the universal laws—illustrated by reincarnation are crucial. Whether or not a soul believes in reincarnation during a particular lifetime is usually unimportant.

Three principles are vital to the worldview of the Cayce readings. Each one is demonstrated by reincarnation as it is described in his material.

1. Life is continuous. Consciousness and personal identity go beyond the grave.
2. God, who created and gives order to the universe, is ultimately just. What may appear to be unfair looks that way only because we cannot see all the factors that are at work in the situation.
3. God loves us and offers us assistance in the long journey of spiritual development. There is not only a law of karma but also a law of grace.

The theory of reincarnation is very significant in helping us to understand those essential principles. However, reincarnation may be merely one of many ways in which those universal truths are revealed. The spiritual laws are much bigger than any theory of rebirth.

Someone who rejects the concept of reincarnation may have found other ways to understand and relate to those key principles. And so in this sense, belief in reincarnation is almost inconsequential according to the Cayce readings. What matters is the here and now. Everything that is ultimately important to spiritual growth is present right now for the soul. In fact, a distorted view of reincarnation could lead someone to become preoccupied with the past, dwelling on useless questions like "Was I once a famous person?" or "Who is my true beloved from past lifetimes?"

This point is made most clearly by one reading Cayce gave on the subject of reincarnation. It was one of those rare readings that was not directed to a single recipient but was a general discourse given for all who might be interested in the subject. This is the finest summary of his position on the theory of rebirth. He stated unequivocally that past lives are a fact, but he also stressed that knowing about them is meaningless unless it makes us better at what we do in the present:

> Only that which produces or makes . . . a citizen a better citizen, a father a better father, a mother a better mother, a neighbor a better neighbor, is constructive.
>
> And to find that [you] only lived, died, and were buried under the cherry tree in Grandmother's garden does not make [you] one whit better [a] citizen, mother or father!

But to know that [you] spoke unkindly and suffered for it, and in the present may correct it by being righteous—that is worthwhile!

What is righteousness? Just being kind, just being noble, just being self-sacrificing; just being willing to be the hands for the blind, the feet for the lame—these are constructive experiences.

[You] may gain knowledge of same, for incarnations *are* a FACT!

How may [you] prove it? In [your] daily living! (5753-2)

If we keep in mind the attitude expressed by this reading, what does the theory of reincarnation say about the meaning of life? First, it suggests that life is purposeful. Everything that happens is for a reason. Because of the choices we have made—minutes ago or even lifetimes ago—we experience either beneficial or troublesome results. A big part of the meaning of life is that we are responsible for ourselves.

Second, reincarnation claims that the situations in which we find ourselves are uniquely suited for spiritual growth. Problems are opportunities to change something about ourselves: an attitude, a feeling, or a behavior. As the Cayce readings often put it, we can make a stumbling block into a stepping-stone.

Finally, the theory of reincarnation states that the purpose of life is ultimately twofold: to make ourselves a little better than we were in the previous lifetime and to make constructive use of the talents we bring with us from past lives. Each of us is born with certain positive characteristics, skills, abilities, sensitivities, and aptitudes. Some of them may require training and persistent efforts in order to blossom, but they all spring from the soul as a carryover from the distant past.

How Could Reincarnation Be True If It's Not in the Bible?

To this question we might respond in a fashion that is apparently glib, but actually quite serious: There are many things in which we "believe" that are not found in the Bible, including electricity and atomic energy. The lack of some topic being included in the Bible should not be used as a case against its validity. Even Jesus himself spoke of there being deeper truths that his followers were not yet prepared to hear and understand.

However, some biblical passages are suggestive of reincarnation or other supportive principles, such as the preexistence of the soul. Proverbs 8:22–35 is a passage into which we might read such a preexistence: "The Lord created me at the beginning of his works, the first of his acts of old. Ages ago I was set up, at the first, before the beginning of the earth" (verses 22–23). If we read the full passage from verse 22 to 35, it becomes clear that the "I" here is defined as "wisdom." But is it wisdom in general or that deeper, inner wisdom with individuality that characterizes the soul? Like so many biblical passages, it can be read and interpreted in more than one way.

Jeremiah 1:5 is a bit more direct in affirming that one's

identity and being may precede physical birth: "Before I formed you in the womb I knew you, and before you were born I consecrated you; I appointed you a prophet of the nations." The Old Testament itself seems to end with a prophecy of reincarnation in Malachi 4:5: "Behold, I will send you Elijah the prophet before the great and terrible day of the Lord comes." It was in reference to this prophecy that Jesus is questioned, "'Then why do the scribes say that Elijah must come?'" His response only thinly veils a direct affirmation of reincarnation, at least in the case of this one soul that had been Elijah: "'I tell you that Elijah has already come, and they did not know him . . .'" Then the biblical account of this scene concludes with such a remarkable statement that only the most forced kind of logic could interpret it as other than reincarnation: "Then the disciples understood that he was speaking to them of John the Baptist" (Matthew 17:10–13).

In another New Testament passage, clear evidence exists that in Jesus's time the possibility was well known that the soul might have had experiences before physical birth. Admittedly such experiences may not have been understood as earthly ones from previous incarnations. In the case of the story of the man born blind, Jesus is asked, "'Rabbi, who sinned, this man or his parents, that he was born blind?'" (John 9:2). Jesus's response does not focus on karmic blame but rather on the creative opportunity of the situation, and he affirms that the purpose of the blindness is to allow the works of God to be manifest, presumably a reference to the fact that Jesus intended to heal the man.

But no matter how we read these and similar passages that

might relate to reincarnation, we are still forced to admit that the thrust of Jesus's own teachings do not seem to include this theory. Nowhere do we find him making such statements as, "Do the best you can in this life, and if you don't quite get it right, you can come back for another chance." We are left to wonder how he could have omitted this teaching if, in fact, it is so central to the way souls work out their spiritual evolution. One option is that a censor at some point in Church history went through the Bible and removed all references to reincarnation. But, as we shall see, the historical record does not support such a conclusion.

Instead, we are left to consider the essential themes of Jesus's ministry. It seems clear that he was more concerned with the present and the future than with the past, so any preoccupation with past lives would seem irrelevant. Although he was very aware of the cultural and religious traditions of his time, he was a teacher of anticipation, of preparation for the End Times. Or at least we may say that those who were around him and recorded his words heard him in this way. They even expected his return in their own lifetime. Of what use is a theory of future incarnations to first-century writers and interpreters of Jesus's life when they expected a final salvation very soon?

What, then, do we know of early Church history and what may have become of thoughts such as the preexistence of the soul and reincarnation? Orthodoxy in the Christian faith did not emerge until the fifth or sixth century. For hundreds of years there were many branches of Christianity, each with its own notion of Christ's teachings, in Egypt, Jerusalem, Asia Minor, Rome, and elsewhere.

One man plays an especially noteworthy role in this saga. In his own times Origen (185–254) was the preeminent theologian of Christianity. Living in Alexandria, on the northern coast of Egypt, he was the first to write a systematic theology of Christianity. By his contemporaries he was called the greatest teacher of the Church after the apostles. He clearly believed in the soul's preexistence; most scholars also interpret his writings to embrace reincarnation. Origen's influence in his own time was great, but we shall see that long after his death he became a key figure in the battle over reincarnation and the Church's relationship to it.

In the fourth century, Christianity entered the political process of the Western world when Constantine adopted it as the state religion. But which of the many branches of Christianity did he select? It was the version of the region in which he lived: Pauline Christianity. Two very significant influences arose from this event. First, we should note that Paul does not seem to have seen reincarnation as being consistent with Christ's teachings. For example, in the letter to the Hebrews, we find this statement: ". . . it is appointed for men to die once, and after that comes judgment" (Hebrews 9:27). Although most scholars do not attribute this letter directly to Paul, it was most likely written by a person from the same circle of thinking as Paul.

The second key influence arising from Constantine's decision concerns the political infighting into which Christianity was drawn. In the centuries following Constantine's reign, the regional authorities of the Church (called bishoprics) attempted to achieve superiority over each other via theological debates. In other words, a measure of political power was gained when the theological position of one city and its bishop could be repudiated in favor of one's own.

By the sixth century certain issues had come to a head, specifically related to bishoprics that claimed to hold positions espoused three hundred years earlier by Origen. The emperor Justinian, in efforts that were probably as much political as theological, attempted to eradicate Origenism. At the Fifth Ecumenical Council in 553, certain decisions were reached to ban teachings of preexistence of the soul. Some modern enthusiasts of reincarnation have claimed that at this council a censor went through the Bible and removed all references to reincarnation. But a careful study of history shows that this is not what happened. However, neither is it accurate to say that the Church unanimously and wholeheartedly rejected reincarnation. Instead, here is what happened at the Fifth Ecumenical Council, according to *The Catholic Encyclopedia*.

(a) With the exception of six bishops from Africa, only the Eastern Roman Empire was represented. There were no representatives from Rome or Western Europe.

(b) The Pope himself was in Constantinople at the time, but was being held captive by Constantine and refused to attend the Council.

(c) The Council was not called to deal with Origen, but with three others whom Justinian thought were heretics. The matter of Origen was taken up in sessions outside the official Council. The actual Council focused on a group in Palestine that claimed to follow Origen but that, in fact, had teachings markedly different from his writings.

(d) The anathemas written by Justinian against Origen were for centuries erroneously assumed to be part of the proceedings of the actual Council.

In other words, Origen's teachings, the clearest example we have of the early Church embracing reincarnation, were retroactively (by some three hundred years) labeled as heretical. Furthermore, this was done for largely political reasons at a council that was not representative of the full Christian world. But before we relegate Justinian to the villain's role in this story, we should keep in mind that by 553 the notion of reincarnation had already become a theory accepted by very, very few Christians. If reincarnation was what Jesus intended to teach (perhaps only to his inner circle), it had been lost around five hundred years after his death. For whatever reason—perhaps because of laypeople's reluctance to accept the personal responsibility inherent in its theory—it was gone.

In conclusion, we must say that reincarnation was not summarily thrown out of the Bible in 553. Rather, we should consider that if it was a part of the living tradition of Christ's teachings, then a certain mind-set of the people caused it to be lost. It is that same mind-set, still alive today, that must be worked with if we are to find a constructive place for this theory in our lives.

DECIDING FOR YOURSELF

Perhaps reincarnation sounds right to you. You may find that it's a powerful aid in making sense of the world around you. On the other hand, you may discover that the theory doesn't feel right or violates important beliefs you hold. If that's the case, you'll probably want to think of your innate talents as God-given rather than the product of past lives. Either way, you can discover your purpose in life by working with the approaches found in this book.

No matter which side you take in the controversy over rebirth, keep this fact in mind: It is *not* the purpose of life to reincarnate. A series of human lifetimes may be one process that your soul follows in order to reach the goal, but reincarnation is not itself your mission. Your true purpose can be found closer to home, in the here and now. Life has meaning because it gives you the chance to discover your true nature and to grow closer to full companionship with God.

Index

ABOUT THE AUTHOR

Mark Thurston, PhD, is an educator, psychologist, and author of more than a dozen books about personal spirituality, dream psychology, meditation, and mind-body well-being. Among his publications are *The Essential Edgar Cayce* (2004) and *Willing to Change: The Journey of Personal Transformation* (2005).

Mark worked for the Association for Research and Enlightenment (A.R.E.) and Atlantic University in Virginia Beach, Virginia, for thirty-six years. In 2009 he moved into a new phase of his own soul's purpose, becoming the director of educational programs for George Mason University's Center for the Advancement of Well-Being. In this capacity his role focuses on teaching undergraduate and graduate courses about consciousness, mindfulness, and the science of well-being.

In 2000 Mark and his wife of many decades, Mary Elizabeth Lynch, cofounded the Personal Transformation and Courage Institute, a nonprofit educational organization that offers small-group learning intensives. Mark and Mary Elizabeth are also the parents of two adult children.

For more information about his work and to contact him via e-mail, visit www.markthurston.com.

About Edgar Cayce and A.R.E.

When Edgar Cayce (1877–1945) was alive and giving readings, one of his dreams was to open a hospital that could offer the many services and remedies that were recommended to the thousands of people who contacted him for help. He had always wanted to help people, and he discovered through his correspondence with those who had received his readings that many of them were having difficulty either finding the recommended remedy ingredients or keeping up with the regimen that was offered in their readings.

In 1928 Cayce's dream of a holistic hospital came true with the opening of the Cayce Hospital for Research and Enlightenment on a sandy dune in the heart of a small coastal fishing town known as Virginia Beach. Unfortunately, after a few years, the hospital closed as a result of financial setbacks during the Great Depression. Cayce's supporters were not deterred. Feeling the need to form an association to continue his great work, in 1931 Cayce and his supporters founded the nonprofit Association for Research and Enlightenment (A.R.E.), which is still in existence today.

With its headquarters located in the same building as the original Cayce Hospital, the A.R.E. provides body-mind-spirit resources for individuals to explore meditation, intuition, dream interpretation, prayer, holistic health, ancient mysteries, and philosophical concepts such as karma, reincarnation, and the meaning of life.

The mission of the A.R.E. is to help people transform their lives for the better, through research, education, and application of core concepts found in the Edgar Cayce readings and kindred materials that seek to promote the purposefulness of life, the spiritual nature and oneness of all life, and the connection of body, mind, and spirit. A.R.E. fulfills this mission with regions and centers throughout the United States and the world, and activities that include conferences, tours, camps for children and adults, regional activities, publishing, and study groups. There are opportunities that allow individuals to engage in self-study as well as gather with like-minded people for education and fellowship worldwide.

A.R.E. offers membership benefits and services that include a quarterly body-mind-spirit magazine, *Venture Inward*, and the *Cayce Quarterly* newsletter, plus exclusive access to the entire set of Edgar Cayce's 14,306 documented readings in an online searchable database.

The association also maintains an affiliation with Atlantic University, which offers continuing education classes and a Master of Arts degree in transpersonal psychology and in leadership studies; the Cayce/Reilly School of Massage, a leader in holistic education, wellness, and health care; and an on-site health center and spa at its Virginia Beach headquarters, where many of the remedies from the health readings are offered in the renovated historic hospital.

To learn more, visit www.EdgarCayce.org.